WADE THE RIVER
DRIFT THE LOCH

*ANGLING
IN SCOTTISH WATERS*

COMPILED BY

R. MACDONALD ROBERTSON
F.S.A.Scot.

OLIVER AND BOYD
EDINBURGH: TWEEDDALE COURT
LONDON: 98 GREAT RUSSELL STREET, W.C.

FIRST PUBLISHED 1948

PRINTED IN GREAT BRITAIN FOR THE PUBLISHERS
BY ROBERT CUNNINGHAM AND SONS LTD., ALVA

M Hewan Crichton
"Cacarach"
Stoer. June 15-22
1953

With
the Author's compliments and best wishes.

R. Macdonald Robertson.

WADE THE RIVER . . . . DRIFT THE LOCH

Dulsie Bridge and the River Findhorn

TO   FIONA

EDITOR'S PREFACE

The charm of scenery is the chief
accessory to the angler's enjoyment.

SIR HERBERT MAXWELL

I THINK I am safe in saying that from the Author's point
of view perhaps the most difficult part in writing a book is
to pen the initial stages in the form of the Preface.

Fishing books—these are legion, and some are new and
some are old, some are good and some are poor. Many give
useful tips and many don't, while others are too highly technical
and tend to bore the reader rather than amuse and interest
him. In compiling this work, however, I have endeavoured
to divert from the usual practice as far as possible, so as to
confine my subject, shall I say, into a mixture of all the fore-
said qualities and conduct my friends on a sporting tour of
the Highlands where recreation, in the form of sport, is not
taken too seriously, and at the same time, offering one or two
useful hints on the theory and practice of casting a line on our
Scottish waters.

In editing this volume, which is essentially constructed
for sportsmen—not " pot-hunters "—I have done so by way
of entertainment more than anything else, and I have endeavoured to do with my pen what the artist does with his
brush.

I have also introduced some folk-lore with the view of
perpetuating some legends of the North which I consider well
worthy of preserving, and I trust I may be excused for doing
so, for there is hardly a river or loch north of the Forth which
does not possess its own supernatural inhabitant, and it is a
true saying that " tradition is a meteor which, if once it falls,
cannot be rekindled ".

While we wade in the cool waters, we often bring ourselves
into parts that have seldom been seen from such points of

view while angling from the bank. It is good therefore, to combine both accomplishments. The mere catching of fish may tire one in time; but the landscape and picturesque rocks, never!

I hope I may lead you while fishing, to think of greater things than killing fish, and to learn that he is a happy man who at times can shake off the cares of this world; and thus enjoy with a contented mind the beauty of nature which is a continual feast at all times.

While I may not have succeeded in presenting any considerable amount of information new to persons well versed in fishing lore, I am sanguine enough to hope that I have succeeded in reproducing a variety of " light and shade " which has not hitherto been bequeathed in a form accessible to brother Anglers.

I have decided to vary my topic in order to cover as much ground as possible within the pages which follow, so as to lend variety, glitter and enchantment to the scenes reminiscent of holidays spent in certain of the more peaceful environment of the Scottish Highlands.

A number of the traditional stories and folk-lore, which I have ventured to include, are translated from the Gaelic and, these being founded on fact, are records of what really is said to have taken place.

In writing this book, it should be clearly understood that with the exception of tidal and navigable waters in which Brown trout fishing alone is free to the public, authority should always be obtained by anglers before commencing to fish Scottish lochs and rivers whether mentioned in this book or not.

I could write a whole volume on West Sutherland alone —a land of foaming mountain streams which plunge over rocky precipices in wild confusion. As far as the eye can see, the moors are encircled by surrounding individual peaks which melt into the sky in the blue haze of the horizon, while below, in places, they give way to pine and birch-clad slopes, which contain numerous lochans, upon whose banks the Royal Fern (*Osmunda Regalis*) grows in profusion.

The Highlander is above all else a kind-hearted natural soul and he, so long as you respect yourself, never forgets to show his respect for you. If you have grassed a stag or landed a salmon in his presence, he will praise you for the rest of your life.

"A fly at one end of the line, and a fool at the other " is the courteous delineation of the angler as he appeared in the eyes of Dr. Samuel Johnson. The Doctor was speaking from his scant knowledge of angling in lazy English waters. He was not familiar with the higher side of the art which can be developed only by him who fishes in the burns which foam and churn their way through our wild and rocky Highland ravines. In such surroundings, notwithstanding his skill, the angler is tried to the utmost, in order to satisfy his thirst to fill the well-worn old-time basket, for fishing in the wilds of Scotland stands aloof, a different proposition to that of casting the line on the tranquil waters of the south, where float fishing is often resorted to with the ubiquitous camp-stool, luncheon basket and the " Sarah Gamp ".

Ever uppermost in the heart of all true sportsmen is the adventure in Scottish burn fishing. In loch fishing from a boat, the same exciting sport does not, in my opinion, exist to the same extent. And what delight and hope springs in the angler's mind when he beholds the first raindrops in response to his prayer that the water may rise.

During the long winter nights when seated around the fire, pipe well alight, turning over the pages of some favourite sporting book, the angler's thoughts instinctively wander through the smoke far away into the hills to his favourite holiday haunts among the ancient bens and glens which he has learned to love so well and where episodes are resurrected and memories awakened which bring that longing to return. As the fisher pours himself out a " tot " he ponders on what it is in fishing which creates this peculiar desire, this fascination and sense of self satisfaction in killing fish? Why should he choose to provide his own food for his table, for example, when fish are generally so plentiful in the shops? The answer is not found in the kill itself, but in the spirit of the chase, and to, but perhaps in a lesser degree, the joys of tramping the heather with rod in hand to reach his favourite haunt.

There are many fishers who have but a limited space of time in Spring to spend in angling, and who seek to know where they may find tolerably good sport without searching for it. Looking for good fishing is not a particularly enviable or profitable way of spending an angling holiday even in Scotland, and when an angler has to pack all his sport into a few days, he certainly cannot afford to waste time in exploration, hence I have not neglected the lighter moods of " the gentle art " for therein lies perhaps half the charm of being an angler. Witness the following stories:

Big Donald the ghillie had endured a hard week's fishing while rowing " the Gentry " on the loch, during the course of which he had been more than amply primed with whisky and other rare vintage, to such an extent that by the time the Sabbath day arrived, he had developed an extremely high blood pressure. His wife becoming seriously alarmed, summoned the local doctor who confirmed that Donald's blood pressure was " enough to burst a barometer ", and prescribed the old-fashioned cure for reducing it, viz., leeches, two of which, he recommended to Big Donald's wife, should be applied to the back of Big Donald's neck. When the doctor returned again to examine his patient a few days later, he enquired how Big Donald was progressing as the result of his prescribed cure, and on asking his wife whether she had carried out his instructions, she replied " Big Donald is just the very same, he is no better or no worse." " But did you not do as I suggested and apply the leeches to the back of his neck? " enquired the doctor, to which his wife replied: "Ach man, God forbid, doctor, as two of those wee craters of leeches wid have been no good whitever to a great muckle monster like Big Donald, I jist clappit two of our ferrets on his neck instead."

The following day was the Sabbath, and the minister in preaching a somewhat lengthy sermon on the evils of drink, said that everyone who over-indulged would surely be condemned to everlasting torture in the Bottomless Pit where

there would be weeping and wailing and gnashing of teeth.
At this juncture, an old woman who was rather overcome with
nerves, got up in a back seat and said: " But minister, I have
just been to our doctor who has pulled all the teeth out of my
mouth."   " Do not worry, my dear lady," said he, " teeth
will be provided."

R. MacDonald Robertson

ACKNOWLEDGMENTS

BEING the Compiler of this Work as well as the Author of a
number of articles contained in its pages, I would like to
express my sincere appreciation to all my friends who have
kindly contributed, directly or indirectly, to this Book.   In doing
so, I should also like to make special reference to the Editors and
Publishers of the following papers who have *inter alia* kindly permitted me to extract certain data from some of my writings which
have appeared in *The Scotsman*, *The Weekly Scotsman*, *The Edinburgh
Evening Dispatch*, *The Edinburgh Evening News*, *The Oban Times* and
The S.M.T. Magazine.

In thanking my many friends and brother anglers who have
co-operated with me in making this book possible, I wish particularly to pay respectful tribute to the late Sir John Fraser, Bart.,
M.C., K.C.V.O., C.B.E., formerly Principal and Vice Chancellor of
the University of Edinburgh for doing me the honour of writing
the Introduction.

My grateful acknowledgments also go out to Mrs. Bessie
Robertson, Pulborough, Sussex; Charles Reid, President of the
Edinburgh City Police Angling Association, and his wife, Mrs.
Reid; Thomas Galloway of the Glasgow City Police Angling
Association; J. H. Campbell of Messrs John Dickson & Son,
Gun-smiths and Fishing-tackle Merchants, Edinburgh; D. J.
Watkins Pitchford, A.R.C.A. (" B.B."); Ian Armstrong, C.A.,
Bettyhill, Sutherland; Sidney Scott, C.B.E., Glasgow; Mrs. Hilda
J. C. Donald, Dundee; V. Carron Wellington, London; The late

Very Rev. John E. Macrae, Dean of Brechin, Angus; Miss M. C. Thorburn, Fishing Tackle Maker, Edinburgh; John G. Ross, Edinburgh; Donald Ross, Ullapool; Donald MacLeod, Kinlochbervie, Sutherland; Murdo MacLeod, Elphin, Sutherland; The Rev. Walter E. Lee, D.D., Edinburgh; Rev. Colonel Alistair Ross, Assistant Chaplain General, H.M. Forces; Rev. Thomas Nicoll Fraser, M.A., Deputy Assistant Chaplain General to H.M. Forces (Highland District), Edinburgh; Samuel MacLean, M.A., Bard to the Gaelic Society of Inverness; John Robertson, Signet Library, Edinburgh; the late Alexander Gunn, Balbreck, Kinlochbervie, Sutherland; John Falconer, Kinlochbervie, Sutherland; Philip Gunn, ex-President, Edinburgh Sutherland Association; W. A. Mackay, President of The Clan Mackay Society, Edinburgh; Charles Jewell, Ben Buie Lodge, Mull; and last but not least, my good friend Gerald F. Baird, F.L.A.S., F.S.I., Secretary of the Loch Lomond Angling Improvement Association, Helensburgh.

Should I have perchance inadvertently omitted the names of any other of my supporters, this has not been my intention.

So far as the illustrations are concerned, I have to express my grateful thanks to Messrs. J. B. White Ltd., Photographic Publishers, Dundee; Donald MacLeod, Kinlochbervie, Sutherland; Lewis Allan, B.Sc., Edinburgh; George D. Donald, Dundee; T. Galloway, Glasgow; and The Rev. Walter E. Lee, D.D., Edinburgh, for granting me the privilege of reproducing their photographic studies herein.

CONTENTS

* Chapters by the Editor

ILLUSTRATIONS

INTRODUCTION

by the late SIR JOHN FRASER, Bart., M.C., K.C.V.O., M.D., LL.D.,
Principal and Vice-Chancellor of the University of Edinburgh.

Of all the world's enjoyments
That ever valued were,
There's none of our employments
With fishing can compare.

THESE LINES from "The Fisherman's Song" in the first part of Massaniello were written nearly 300 years ago. To-day they are echoed by a company as the sands of the sea in number, those who find pleasure in the gentle sport of angling.

The moralist will say that there are two sides to this question; that which spells enjoyment to the fisher is apt to mean disaster for the fish. The logic of the argument is beyond dispute, but in fairness let it be said that the scales (forgive the pun) are not weighted unduly in the human's favour. Any angler worthy of the name will tell you that he has a profound respect for the instinct displayed by his friend the fish. Indeed I had almost written the word intelligence, in expressing the piscine reaction to a lure. I know that to use the term would have incurred the criticism of the philologists; none the less, when one has exhausted all one's art and energies in attempting to persuade the dwellers in the waters that some of the most edible and attractive members of the ephemeral kingdom are within their grasp and yet the basket remains empty, it is difficult to divorce oneself from the feeling that there is being made manifest, to one's discomforture, a discrimination which is akin to intelligence; and if this estimate would seem to set too high a standard we may find comfort in the reflection that it may be crass stupidity, and in the last resort, spite! I mention these points in support of my contention that the game is a reasonably fair one; that the chances of the fish are equal to and perhaps better than those of the fisher.

But to hook the fish is only part of the joy of angling. There is the " setting "—and how much it means! The charm of earth's open spaces, where the loch nestles beneath the shadow of the mighty ben; where the burn burbles its way through the windings of the lonely glen, and the broad majestic river adds its music to the chorus of field and copse and dell. These are the scenes in which memories find root— and what happy and precious memories they are—of long summer days in a green and pleasant countryside; of evenings when the golden twilight passes so gently into a scented dusk. It is true that impressions such as these are so much the happier if the " catch " be a good one; but even if the luck be against us and the basket is light, or even empty, pictures have been painted upon the tablets of memory, pictures which will never fade but which instead grow brighter and more appealing as the years slip by.

" Wade the River, Drift the Loch " may be described as a fishing anthology in prose. Mr. Macdonald Robertson, as editor-in-chief, is responsible for the general arrangement of the volume, and, as is proper, his facile pen has written a number of the articles contained therein. But the book is the outcome of a community effort inspired by the team spirit, and thus it is that he has been assisted by a number of his fishing friends, each of whom has recalled in words memories of days and nights such as only anglers know. The result is altogether delightful: a storehouse replete with impressions where there are mingled together in most pleasant vein the thrill which sport affords, the peace of spirit which belongs to the countryside. This is a book to read in wintertime, when the rods are packed away and the fly-book lies unopened; it is at such a time that we dream of the hours which have passed, that we look forward to the days which are to come. Within the pages of " Wade the River, Drift the Loch," you will find that which will help you to indulge in both exercises. I know no better tonic for a flagging spirit or a weary mind.

BONNIE STRATHARDLE

O Bonnie Strathardle!
   Glen of my heart!
Thou art calling me back
   From the great world's mart.

The river that runs
   O'er its shingly bed,
The haunt of the angler,
   Where rowans grow red.

The road that winds onwards,
   Past cottage and hall,
To the quaint little village,
   Kirkmichael, queens all.

The bridge o'er the Ardle,
   Close by the Churchyard,
Where sleep their departed,
   To reap their reward.

The strains of the pipes
   On the still evening air,
In Bonnie Strathardle
   Have naught to compare.

It recalls to my mind
   The ancient of days,
When the clansmen rose up,
   In their bonnets and plaids.

When the river ran red
   With the blood that was shed
In Bonnie Strathardle,
   The shades of the dead.

Thy beauty and charm
   For aye will abide,
O Bonnie Strathardle!
   A fair country-side!

MARGARET REID

CHAPTER I

FISHING IN STRATHARDLE

by CHARLES REID

THE Ardle flows in an easterly direction, winding from its sources in bleak and high-lying regions, passing through a pastoral country, becoming more highly cultivated and populous, on its way to join the Blackwater where it forms the Ericht. The two principal tributaries of the Ardle in its upper reaches are the Brierachan and the Fernate. The Brierachan rises near Loch Valigan at the foot of Ben-y-Gloe and joins the Fernate to form the Ardle. Its length is about twelve miles and it affords good burn-trout fishing in April, May, August and September. The majority of the trout are smallish owing to the boulder strewn nature and the mountainous course through which this stream wends its way, but an occasional big fellow may be met with, in some of the pools. The Fernate rises on the rocky summit of a hill in Glenfernate and falls into the Brierachan. It is also a brawling mountain stream with a run of about five or six miles and yields good trout fishing. The trout average five or six to the pound. In dry and sunshiny weather they are stiff to move, the bottom of the stream generally being of light-coloured rock, but when swollen, and the spate clearing off with a fair breeze, a good angler will speedily fill his basket with average trout. Worm is more deadly than fly. When the water is small and clear, a long rod and short line is necessary. The scenery of this glen is very fine.

The river Ardle is a first-rate trouting stream, and most of it is generally open to the respectable and civil angler. Some stretches above Bridge of Cally are preserved, but there too, leave may often be obtained, if it be courteously asked. Capital trout fishing is to be had all along its course, which

flows through a very pretty glen, among grassy hills and
grouse moors. The trout average from three to eight ozs.
but frequently a pounder is met with in the deep pools.
From May to September is the best season, when good baskets
can be obtained. The village of Kirkmichael nestles on both
sides of its banks and an ideal centre from which the angler
can go fishing. There are two first-class Hotels and many
houses in the village where rooms may be secured. As I
recall it, about the middle of its course, it is already of some
width. To the eye of the fisherman it is a perfect stream,
deep pools break into foaming rapids which again flow on in
glassy glides, throughout diversified by boulders and stones,
great and small. The Ardle is noted as being one of the most
prolific of trout streams, excelling not only in the number, but
also in the beauty of its trout. It is a sight to be remembered
when on some fine day in spring one happens to be witness of
a great hatch of March Browns or May-fly. The surface of
the water is broken by a constant succession of rings as the
hungry trout suck down the delicate morsels as they emerge
for a brief moment on the surface, for many of them their
life-span may well, indeed, be termed ephemeral. I recall
whole days spent on this one portion, with the result that the
pressure of the basket strap on shoulder, hinted that enough
had been done for sport and pleasure, for be it noted, for the
full enjoyment of one's river one must be alone. To me, as
a stream upon whose banks I was born and brought up, the
Ardle is particularly dear, and, indeed, there is hardly a hole
or corner in the river with which I am unacquainted. During
the course of forty years I have fished many rivers mostly in
the south and midlands of Scotland, but no stream gives me
more pleasure than a day on my favourite Ardle. One
morning in early May a few years ago, I set off from the
village in which I was holidaying for a few hours fishing. It
was a beautiful morning with a very slight east wind and a
few light clouds overhead. On reaching a pool about a mile
below the village where the Balwald burn joins the parent
river, I decided to make a start. The river was slightly above
normal level and of a light gin colour. I sat down on the

bank for a few minutes by the side of the river and smoked a cigarette, while I carefully watched to see if any flies were on the water in order to select a cast. As no fish were rising at the moment and no flies could be observed, I decided to make up a cast of March Brown, Greenwell Glory and Partridge and Yellow and commenced fishing at the tail end of the pool. I had only made a few casts when suddenly the pool became boiling with rising fish. I never saw anything like this before, nor in fact since, the trout simply jumped over one another in their eagerness to get the flies which had just hatched. I did not take time to investigate which fly had hatched out, being kept so busy taking out fish with all three flies which I had already on my cast. The rise lasted for fully half an hour and ceased as suddenly as it started. However, during that period, I hooked and landed twenty-seven trout out of that pool, all of takeable size. On two occasions during the rise, I hooked and landed three trout at once. There are many fine pools and streams on the Ardle and, provided the day is suitable, many good baskets of trout can be obtained by the angler.. In conclusion, I can only remark that from my own widespread experiences, the angler who obtains leave for a good fishing day, will assuredly enjoy a charming outing at his favourite pastime when engaged upon the banks of this pretty little river whose praises I have so feebly sung.

CHAPTER II

LONELY SHORES

by THOMAS GALLOWAY

ODE TO A COTTAGE IN STRATHFILLAN

I know a cottage on the purple moor,
 Where all day long, the lonely curlews cry,
And round it in the night-time, ceaselessly,
 The soft winds sigh:
And there's peace, peace, peace,
 In earth and air and sky.

There the cares that crowd the busy hour,
 Fade soft away like some far clarion call,
And those wild fears that come at twilight-time,
 No more appal;
And there's sleep, sleep, sleep,
 When the long grey shadows fall.

THE June sun was still high in the sky, when, having dined well at Tigh-na-Struith (The House of the River) I meandered along the Tyndrum road towards Inverhaggernie Burn. In days gone by, I had often studied a map of the district and especially a patch of blue—Loch Maragan —situated about three miles distant from Crianlarich, over two hills, a loch which I had so far never visited. However, I had taken the precaution to obtain local advice as to the best way of proceeding there, and now I was determined to give it a little attention.

About one mile up the road, I turned right and, following a cart track, I crossed the Fillan River at the wooden bridge. Several nice trout were rising to flies in the stream below, but I could only afford a casual glance, as I hurried on. By-

4

passing the small farm resting at the foot of lovely Glen Inverhaggernie, I climbed the left brae of the hillside, through bracken reaching to the waist. Far below, I saw the burn cascading over monstrous boulders into dark mysterious pools. I could actually picture, in the long ago, that Thor, the God of Thunder, had cast his thunderbolt at this spot, so devastating is the wild scenery of this glen; long fissures show in the hillside and massive rocks poise, seemingly ready to tumble down into chaos below. Nevertheless, the fearless angler treads his perilous way up the waterside, jumping from rock to rock, just for the pleasure of fishing the next pool. Certainly this stream holds many trout, small, no doubt, but very sporting.

About one mile up the glen, I saw the fence stretching away to the right, so down I slid, scrambled across the burn, and climbing, reached the fence. A narrow path winds along through bog and moor, past small round peaty pools, where one must tread with care. After a somewhat tedious, but invigorating hike, I struggled over a last mound and there below, stretched Loch Maragan . . . at last!

This loch is about half a mile long and very narrow, with a small island at the eastern extremity. Fishing therein is reputed to be very good and, if one is fortunate to obtain permission to do so, a good basket should easily be obtained provided, of course, that the conditions are favourable.

On the southern shore, I espied an angler plying his rod, his cast flashing in the sunlight. I sat down and watched his action. A cool breeze just wrinkled the water's surface, but no fish were on the move. The angler wound in his line and passed the time of day with me—he did look disgusted and no wonder, as he summed up the position with the word " Hopeless ". I smilingly suggested that he should try the northern shore, he shrugged himself in agreement and together we walked along the pebbly strand. At a little bay, half covered with reeds, I asked him to try his luck, to throw out his line and draw his flies towards the reeds, it looked a likely spot. The flies danced lightly on the water, there was an immediate swirl and the reel screamed protest, the fish bored deeply and then rushed towards the reeds, but my friend skilfully turned him just in time. Out went the butt, the fish rushed out again, jumped high in the air and lashed out with his powerful tail, but down came the rod and off he rushed again, but not so boldly, he was weakening, he turned, his golden body gleaming in the light of the setting sun; gently he was pulled shorewards and dragged upon the shingle—a lovely pounder. My friend smiled.

We crossed a beautiful green sward, picking our way gingerly, over a treacherous bog, and round a small knoll, when suddenly the stillness of the evening calm was shattered with the strident screaming of hundreds of seagulls. On a muddy promontory nearby, we discovered many gulls, nesting, we presumed. Our untoward intrusion had, no doubt, disturbed their domestic tranquillity. How the birds wheeled and dived; I believe that I squirmed and that my friend muttered something, scarcely audible to the human ear.

Far out on the loch, several cruiser trout were scouting around, sucking down blaes, their large dorsal fins continuously breaking the surface. There is no boat on this loch and so I was left to well-wishing that perchance the fish would drift closer to the shore. However my friend kept his flies on the water and his patience was rewarded from time to time and his catch mounted up.

In my opinion, the dry fly fisher could profit well on this water. But why dry fly? Well, I had been watching the fish rising to the natural flies and they seemed to be swimming just below the surface, ready to pounce on the unwary fly as it momentarily struck the water. I told my friend to tie a dry fly on the bob, which he did. Before re-casting, and while drawing off more line, his cast inadvertently dropped on the water's surface close into the shore, there was a sudden swirl, the fly on the bob disappeared, a big trout had made a big mistake; off he bolted to the deeps, taking out about twenty yards of line, but my friend soon had him under control and very soon another pounder was added to the basket.

Many a good fish fell to the bob that evening, before my friend thought that he had had enough sport for this outing.

PLATE II

The River Fillan, near Tyndrum

The evening light was fading in the west, when we set off from Loch Maragan. Another outing had ended, but perhaps on some not too distant day, I will return to this beautiful spot, and myself, enjoy a glorious evening's sport with the Maragan " brownies ".

I left my friend soon after and cut across the moors, through a wilderness of lichens and mosses, over peaty quagmires, and down to where the Inverhaggernie burn rises, near Lochan Dubh. This small tarn is dark brown in colour, but how pleasant to watch the golden gleam of the nymphing trout; not far off to the right lies Loch Essan, reputed for its trout, and Lochan Chailan, which feeds the River Lochay. This latter lochan holds numerous trout, little brownies, bold risers to the fly. But unfortunately no approach can be made to the lochan except at the point where the feeder stream enters, due to the dangerous condition of the banks, which are floating morasses. Local information given suggests that there are many three pounders in tenancy of the middle deeps of this water, but on the occasion that I fished there, I am afraid that the big ones were having a nap.

I followed Inverhaggernie downwards for many a weary mile, entranced with the surrounding scenery . . . cascading waterfalls, enchanting pools shaded with lonesome birch trees, until the beautiful valley of Strathfillan came into view. It is indeed an excellent sight that one obtains, a panorama of rugged hills stretching away to the blue distance, and the visitor to this locality is amply rewarded for his pains in attaining this vantage point.

Thereafter the journey back to Crianlarich presents no difficulties and soon I was at home, lolling back in my armchair, recalling the happy hours spent in the hills, and wondering when again I should see Loch Maragan.

The angler, while visiting this part of Perthshire, should not miss the opportunity of casting a line on Lochs Iubhair and Dochart, the latter small loch containing many half pounders with an occasional big one. If one is fortunate to be there during the period, middle of June until August, then one can perhaps deceive the lordly salmon, as he rests awhile, before pursuing his arduous journey up the Fillan to the shingly spawning beds, where it was given life. Loch Dochart, although weedy in parts, gives excellent sport in the evenings, when the light is just failing; the fish are bold risers and especially when the flies are dancing close to the boat. One is apt then to be off guard, the line is slack, the fish takes, and as they are expert at ejecting the hook, it is a common occurrence to lose many fish before one is safely creeled . . . so keep that line taut and your mind from wandering. One point of interest to all visitors to this locality, is the double echo (a remarkable phenomenon) which returns from the " Deil's Prison " and the grim precipitous, rocky shore on the north side of the loch and often affords amusement to parties visiting the island. Permission must be obtained locally to land on this island, on which stands the ruins of a castle, said to be the earliest residence of the Campbells of Glenfalloch and the first haven of refuge sought by Bruce after his first untimely reverse at Methven, near Perth.

CHAPTER III

LOCH ERRICHT

by R. MACDONALD ROBERTSON

LOCH ERRICHT, a long narrow sheet of water extending from Dalwhinnie in Inverness-shire, is about 15 miles in length by approximately 1 mile in breadth and lies almost due north and south in contrast to nearly all the principal lochs of Perthshire, which all lie practically east and west, with the exception of Loch Lubnaig, and every one of these lochs, apart from Loch Erricht, have more than one feeding stream entering their waters at their head. Loch Erricht is unique, having no head stream flowing into it at its upper end other than a few small rills which issue in wet weather from a mossy swamp round the head of the Loch.

Loch Erricht, which is conveniently fished from Dalwhinnie Hotel, about one mile distant, forms the extreme north-west portion of the parish of Fortingall and the County of Perth-shire, although a part of the Loch is situated in Inverness-shire. It is one of the great chain of Perthshire lochs and lies at an elevation of some 1,200 feet above sea level. The scenery round about is wild and gloomy, presenting lonely windswept shores and the mountains on either side rise sheer up from the water's edge in savage grandeur, their sides being deeply scarred by boulder strewn gullies the summits of which are composed of lofty pinnacles. Along the east bank are rocks and stunted foliage and on the west side stands Ben Alder, about six miles down from the head of the Loch. Its bare perpendicular cliffs tower majestically upwards to a height of 3,766 feet, and on the face is a cave, in which Prince Charles Edward Stuart is said to have taken refuge after his disastrous defeat at Culloden. The only habitation is a shooting lodge situated in a secluded neuk. The Loch is said to be of immense depth in several places. Its waters extend so close to the summit level of the comparatively small ridge which separates it from the River Truim (one of the head tributaries of the Spey) that there is practically no area for water to drain or collect. I have never actually rowed all the way to the foot of the Loch, but for a good many miles down I did not notice a single stream of any consequence entering the water; but I am informed the only feeder of any consequence falls into the Loch a good distance down. There is a keeper's cottage about three miles from the lower end and half a mile inland, where anglers have been known to find accommodation over night.

Generally speaking, Loch Erricht is reckoned a good loch for *salmo ferox*; but in my experience, the trout I caught on the fly were only fair sized fish averaging about half a pound, though good fighters. Should the angler decide on fly fishing, advantage should be taken of the first favourable breeze in order to drift to the lower end of the Loch, making every allowance for a possible detention of one or two days should the wind increase! Should this involve no hardship, it will offer to the fisher an opportunity of testing the water in various moods.

Trolling from the north end is reckoned to be good for a distance of about eight miles. Two rods are recommended with lines of about 100 yards in length, on the end of which single wire swivel traces with lead sinkers and tackles should be attached. Natural minnows are the best lures, or small trout secured on archer spinners of appropriate size. As the Loch is very deep at this part, two ounce sinkers will not prove too heavy. For this purpose trout of about four inches long may easily be obtained from the Truim, which flows at the back of the Hotel. Trolling should be performed in zig-zag fashion, the critical " taking time " being at the turn of the boat, as the lures swing round, and rowing should not be too slow. Care should be taken to ensure that the bait spins smoothly, and it should be inspected at regular intervals to see that it is in working order and not weeded up.

Once the sandy bay of Corrievrachie has been reached,

trolling should be discontinued, and fly fishing resorted to for the southern journey back to the head of the Loch. Every few yards of comparative shallow is intersected by sudden dips into patches of deep dark water, on the ledges of which, given a soft sky with a drizzle of rain and a gentle breeze blowing up the Loch, a good basket may usually be secured. Ordinary Loch Leven size of flies will do fine; but I recommend a cast of either Palmers or Pennells with a worm fly (with red or orange tip) on the tail. If the breeze be strong, however, I recommend March Browns, Woodcock and Yellow, Grouse and Claret, Teal and red, Blue and Black and Zulus, a trifle larger than those used on Loch Leven, not forgetting the worm fly, already referred to; but in such circumstances a size slightly larger.

One day, in company with a friend, I had the good fortune to land a *ferox* about midway down the Loch. As luck would have it, the breeze suddenly changed which aided our drift homeward. A somewhat peculiar feature of this Loch is that if you get a wind at all, you are greatly independent of direction, and should the breeze blow up or down the water you may calculate on drifts of about two miles in extent when good results may be expected; but if the drift be across the Loch, you drift over a series of gravelly banks or ridges, and occasionally between them, where trout sometimes take, especially in the vicinity of the keeper's cottage already mentioned.

The wind suddenly seemed to increase from a moan to a whistle blowing down the side of Ben Alder in a perfect hurricane, leaving us no alternative but to go before it, steadying our pace with the oars, while all around us were creamy white waves. Suddenly, off went the reel on one of our rods with a sharp screech, causing the point of the rod to twitch in convulsive movements. Immediately, I seized my rod which bent like a willow branch under the strain, as foot after foot of line unwound itself from the reel drum. "Air-chinnte ire Muem hora-Mhor tha aige an duine" shouted our boatman as the line shot out, just as the fish rose out of the water about 150 yards away, in a gigantic leap for freedom. Then the

line suddenly slackened; but suddenly tautened again, as the
fish dived down to the inky depths. By this time my friend
was busy winding in the line on the other rod as fast as he
could, in order to prevent entanglement, as the trout tugged
and pulled like the very devil, while my rod bent like a hook.
After a few mad rushes the big trout gradually came to the
surface with a sudden swirl, which enabled me to wind in
several more yards of line and after a few more runs and
plunges, I got him near the boat which was pitching badly,
while our ghillie struggled to row against the rolling waves.
At any moment, I expected my sullen captive to make a
sudden spring; but he did not, and I saw that his strength
was slowly beginning to weaken. With difficulty and no
small risk, having shipped the oars, our ghillie seized the gaff
and stood up ready to strike. At length, as I manoeuvred
the *ferox* past the stern of the boat, our boatman cleeked him
very skilfully; but the boat giving a sudden lurch, the gaff
broke, leaving the greater part of the shaft in his hand, and
off went the fish in another wild rush down into the depths.
The dilemma now was how to secure him! My companion
at once ordered the ghillie to keep the prow steady against the
gale, and in this fashion allow the boat to drift towards the
nearest sheltered bay on the shore, which on reaching, my
friend leapt overboard amidst the foam and raced along the
bank until he reached a comparatively smooth sandy creek.
After a somewhat prolonged battle with the elements and the
fish, I managed to bring him near the shore where my friend
was waiting. Suddenly, the big trout, being badly wounded
and quite exhausted as the result of the prolonged struggle,
turned over on its side and being carried on the curling crest
of a big wave was left, by a second receding wave, high and
dry on the sandy inlet and after heaving the monster up the
bank an end was soon put to its sufferings by my friend.

On landing, we weighed the fish on a pocket scales—just
under $8\frac{3}{4}$ lbs.—one of the ugliest black looking specimens
which I have ever seen, with large head and vicious mouth—
hardly suitable for exhibition in a museum.

I am informed that in the extreme west end corner of the

Loch there is a patch of yellowish sand, where trout of excellent quality and colour markings can be caught. In this quarter of the Loch baskets up to thirty fish in a day, averaging half a pound, are not uncommon, although much heavier baskets have been recorded from this part of Loch Erricht.

Would space allow, there is much one could write concerning the natural wonders of this unfrequented district, in which the golden eagle and peregrine falcon still soar in the heavens above the Loch.

There is a legend concerning the original formation of this weird Highland Loch. According to the tradition, the whole area now covered by water was at one time a populated valley which formed a parish named Feadail. In the course of one night, it is said, after the inhabitants had retired to sleep a partition to some huge subterranean body of water was suddenly burst open by a terrific convulsion of Nature, when the whole parish was submerged, and all the inhabitants along with their crofts, fields, horses and cattle were overwhelmed and drowned. The traditional story also bears out that "for long afterwards the church and several other prominent objects were to be seen on a clear summer day far down at the bottom of the Loch."

CHAPTER IV

SOME TIPS ON FISHING HIGHLAND LOCHS

by R. MACDONALD ROBERTSON

I N LOCH fishing trout can safely be regarded as psychic, for they seem actually to sense the moment when the angler's thoughts are distracted.

In fishing from a boat a great deal depends upon (1) casting a long and delicate line at rapid intervals, dropping the flies lightly on the water, allowing them to rest on the surface only for a very short time; (2) altering the speed at which the flies should be drawn through the water to suit the circumstances, viz., when there is no ripple and the water is calm, it is wise to sink the flies and draw them slowly through the water, never towards the centre of the boat; but out towards each end of it. When there is a moderate breeze the tail fly should be allowed to sink slightly and the bob fly tip the surface. In a strong breeze, it is advisable to draw the flies more quickly through the waves, as the fish in such circumstances usually lie nearer the surface. Better results are usually had by drawing the flies through the water more quickly in the afternoon than in the morning.

One should never be in too great a hurry to strike a fish; the strike should be operated, if possible, as the trout turns. Should you observe a fish lunging for the flies, try to draw them away from him with a sharp, quick lift of the rod. A turn of the wrist is enough.

Herein lies the trick, for you are not quick enough to pull the flies away from the trout, but the jerk of the line usually has the desired effect of embedding the hook in the mouth of the fish; but be careful how you play him in case he frees the hook, and keep a steady strain on him, as the least bit of slack line affords him a chance to tear loose.

In angling, it is essential to keep one's eye on the line. In nearly all forms of sport, accuracy produces results, and in fishing, a strike made at the psychological moment wins the prize.

Should there be a series of quick, nervous rises, this generally indicates that the trout are nymphing, and in such circumstances it is often advisable to slightly trim the flies with a pair of scissors.

By using a tapered cast, one is liable to cause the flies to drop on the water in a more convincing manner, and when casting, one should try to paralyse one's line in mid air, causing it to drop lightly and almost helplessly on the water. After a little practice this method of casting becomes perfectly simple.

In loch fishing it is an important matter to study the wind for fish generally lie along the shore on which the breeze blows; at least grilse and sea trout usually do, and if the wind is blowing hard, they lie close inshore.

If you ever get into difficulties with a boat on rough water and you find the wind and the tide run so fast that they frustrate all your efforts to battle against them, make a bee-line for the bank and continue on your way by hugging the shore. If even by so doing, your journey appears longer, it pays in the end, as you always get to your destination far safer and in a quicker space of time than you would by struggling up the middle of the loch in the teeth of the wind.

It is often quite worth while trying a cast under trees on banks which overhang the loch, even on calm days when one's flies should be allowed to sink slightly. Once a trout is hooked it is wise principle to bring it to the net as soon as possible.

On bright sunny days a pair of tinted sun-goggles is an advantage as they help to relieve glare and assist in seeing when to strike a rising fish. On such occasions, when there is little or no breeze and the sun is merciless, I recommend casting as far out of the track of the boat as possible, sinking the flies, letting them descend within the observation of the fish, then drawing them back in a series of slow jerks, causing them to resemble the movements of the acquatic insects

beneath the surface. Try as far as possible never to let your
gut dry in the sun's rays. Once the gut is wet it should
remain so until the day's fishing is completed. For bright
sunny weather I recommend dying the gut a blue-black
colour to prevent glitter, or stain the gut dark tea colour.
Gently rubbing the gut with rubber will remove its polish.

The great secret of loch fishing is not to be discouraged.
Keep on casting and try to keep the flies in the water as much
as possible.

The loch fisher is dependent upon the wind to curl the
surface of the water and on a small loch the angler has often
a blank day on account of lack of sufficient breeze. In river
fishing, on the other hand, the angler depends largely on the
condition of the water in order to fill his basket. Therefore,
providence controls in either case what is usually termed a
" good " day; but experience has taught me that the " good "
days are usually few and far between.

In loch fishing the boatman is mainly responsible for the
success of the fisher. An angler who is not conversant with
the stretch of water he is fishing, may waste his energy casting
all day without result; therefore it is advisable to hire the
services of a local boatman who knows all the best stretches
and bays of the loch.

So far as equipment is concerned, light-coloured clothes
should be avoided, as the eyesight of a fish is the keenest sense
which it possesses, and on a clear fine day there is no doubt
that an unusual white object within range of its vision, will
cause a fish to turn-tail and make off into the depths or cause
the trout to rise short of the fly.

In loch fishing, the creel should be of the largest size made
so as to serve for all kinds of fish and if the angler is using a
boat, there is ample room to accommodate it. The basket-
work should last a long time if the edges and the bottom are
bound with leather. Metal hinges will also be found a great
advantage. A fishing bag is also a very convenient article;
but unless the waterproof cloth, with which it is lined, is
carefully washed periodically, a nasty smell is apt to be
contracted and retained. The landing net should have a good

PLATE III

The Shore, the Mid and the Deep Rods—used in fishing a Highland loch

A delightful ripple on a Highland loch

long handle attached to it, and the net should be made of stout twine which prevents entangling and the hoop of a size capable of landing a big fish. The universal screw on the end of the pole should also be able to fit a gaff hook when it is necessary to substitute the one for the other.

As much has already been written in regard to size of rods, I do not intend to labour this point, as there are so many varied opinions in the matter; but an angler will be well advised to take a spare rod in the boat with him in case of calamity. The rod should not bend too freely, and a split cane one (with or without a steel centre) is an ideal article. For loch fishing all fancy rods should be avoided, and it is well worth paying a little extra for a hall-marked make. The angler should always carry a couple of reels, the smaller with say 60 to 70 yards of fine line and the larger with not less than 100 yards of stouter variety. Care should be taken before commencing fishing operations to see that the line runs freely on the reel-drum and that it does not possess any kinks or flaws. When buying rods, it is essential to have reels fitted to them properly to make certain that they fit securely, for nothing is more annoying to have a reel tumble off the rod while playing a fish.

I am not much in favour of hook-books as they are a great temptation to keep too large a stock of old flies. Flies and gut in a fly book are apt to get crushed and moistened with the weather, and I hold that the best receptacles for holding tackle are moderately sized flat tin boxes such as cigarettes are sold in. For a day's fishing, only take as many flies and spare casting lines as you think necessary and, if possible, ascertain beforehand the size most suitable for the loch in which you intend to fish. One or two casts of flies of different sizes should be made up before starting operations according to the weather conditions and it is usually advisable to take the advice of the ghillie on this subject especially if he is well acquainted with the loch. I shall refrain from giving a detailed list of flies as the choice of these should fall to the discretion of the angler, and I have always found the usual Loch Leven size, which most fly traders know about well, serves the

c

purpose for trout fishing. It is a matter of opinion whether single or double fly hooks are best. Tinsel is a very useful addition to a fly hook, especially in loch fishing. Flies should not be tied on too fine gut as they are apt to get twisted round the casting line. The colours of flies on a cast should be varied as much as possible. One should provide oneself with one or two casting lines of different thicknesses. For a day's loch fishing, according to the circumstances of the weather and having regard to whether the angler intends to fish for trout, salmon or sea trout, it is advisable to have gut stained (for example tea colour) before setting out. Casts should not be more than three yards long at the most and it is not advisable to fish with more than three flies at a time, especially if there is a stiff breeze blowing. Three flies on a cast should cover as much water as any number of flies. I shall not enter into the subject of tying or knotting tackle as most fishermen have their own theories and methods of joining tackle together. Further, this point is widely laid down in many standard works on the subject.

Trolling should never be resorted to if one can get results with the fly. There is neither the same skill nor real enjoyment in the mere killing of fish on the troll. A well-known writer once said: " It is a most unsportsmanlike proceeding to take fish on the grapnel," but there are occasions when trolling is excusable, such as when fly fishing is proved to be perfectly useless.

Fair trolling, however, is quite legitimate and in many cases it is quite a usual practice to troll if the basket is to be filled at all, as some days the fly is of no use—due either to a bright sky or a dead calm; but trolling with either artificial or natural bait is a far less exciting sport than fly fishing. In trolling, a rod specially adapted for the purpose should be used in order to avoid strain on the ordinary fly rod. The trolling rod need not be longer than about 12 feet, but it must be stiffish and the rings through which the line is led should be of large diameter, standing out prominently from the wood (upright rings). In trolling, the reels should be of large dimension and capable of holding at least 100 yards of line.

The line should be as strong as possible and of a kind which will not readily kink. The troller should provide himself with minnow traces. These do not require to be more than two yards long, but the swivels should be sufficiently large to ensure the bait (natural or artificial weighted or unweighted minnow) spinning nicely. Traces can usually be made out of strands of thin piano wire and swivels are usually procured from most tackle shops. I have found that a single wire trace has its distinct advantages, especially on clear days; but care should be taken to see that the wire does not become kinked, as this often causes a severance when any strain is applied to it thereafter. The easiest way to carry wire traces is to coil them round a circular piece of wood about four inches in diameter. This lessens the chances of the wire becoming kinked.

There is often a difficulty in catching minnows. The methods of catching minnows are already well known and I do not wish to elaborate unduly the ways and means of catching them with nets and jars, etc. The Parr-tail is a deadly bait for salmon; but in prior articles I have been condemned for mentioning this mode of fishing and therefore, valuable bait as it may be, I will refrain from advocating the use of this lure.

In launching minnows it is most important to keep the boat moving at a steady pace and to see that they spin easily before attempting to let out line. The line should be released carefully in proportion to the speed of the boat to prevent the hooks fouling the bottom. In trolling, one should always take a supply of split swanshot for use when it is desired to sink line and minnow below surface. An archer-spinner is the most suitable tackle to use for a natural bait. The size and colour of the minnow should depend upon a number of conditions—principally the nature of the fish which one intends to catch. A bright coloured minnow is usually chosen for a bright day and a dark coloured one for a dull day; but this is, of course, a matter of opinion. A spoon bait is also a very excellent lure and there are many other spinning devices which act as a splendid deception, but which I need not elaborate.

In most lochs, trolling with two rods will be found ample, although in lochs such as Loch Ness and Loch Shiel the custom is to use three trolling rods at once (the " shore," the " mid " and the " deep "). The " shore " and the " deep " rods should be held or placed at right angles to the boat and the " mid " should rest longways out behind the stern. Care should be taken to see that the butts of the rods are well secured so as to prevent any of the rods from going overboard on a fish being hooked. It is a good idea to place the rods in hold-fasts between two pieces of cork, which have nails driven through them longways, securing them to the gunwale of the boat, looping their butts to the seats with a piece of string in such a way that they are held firm and their reels are able to run freely on the indication of a tug. The line between the reel and the first eye on the rod should be eased in slightly on top of the seat and a sufficiently heavy stone placed on it as a check to take up the strain and to prevent the taut line from causing the reel to unwind as the boat continues on its course. The sudden clatter of the stone from off the seat, combined with the screech of the reel, usually denotes that the minnow has become fast in something what-ever it may be. In trolling, plenty of line should be let out —never less than thirty yards. Each rod should have a different length of line for, should the fish not seize the first lure, he may seize the second or third. As natural minnow is more apt to get out of order than the artificial kind, one should see that the bait is intact and that it spins properly by hauling it in periodically for examination. Trolling should be conducted in zig-zag fashion and the minnow should be swung, rather than trolled into bays. Turning the boat entails a considerable circle being taken in order to keep the baits spinning and so prevent the lines getting mixed up. As soon as a fish is hooked, the other rod or rods should be reeled in as quickly as possible, and if the fish, which is hooked, needs playing, the rod on which it has come should be seized without delay. To avoid the risk of a serious tangle I advise the use of reels of large diameter. On days when casting is unproductive, results may often be obtained by trolling

ordinary casts of flies behind the boat. In fact, fishing with
fly and minnow can quite easily be done at the same time.
One thing novel, if trolling with minnows, is that the best
size of fish are generally got by this means, and this is one
way of ridding a loch of cannibal fish which cause great havoc
among the other species.

One is fortunate if one can obtain the service of a good
and reliable boatman. Some boatmen are past masters in
the art of landing fish and extricating the hook in record
time, as also freeing lines should they have become tangled
up. It is indeed a pleasure to be out all day in the company
of a native man at the oars, but some ghillies row the boat in
a slipshod manner and a day in such company is something
which one does not care to look back upon with any feeling
of satisfaction. The boatman should always be in sympathy
with the angler and enable him to cover as much water as
possible with his flies and endeavour to cause him that expectant
rise at every cast, whether it should materialise or not. With
such a boatman, instructions regarding the management of
the craft are superfluous, but when one is in the hands of a
boatman who is not too *au fait* with his work, one requires
to give him a few hints. It is a good precaution to see that
everything is in order before setting off and all unnecessary
tackle put out of the way and to have the landing-net or gaff
conveniently ready for use. It will usually be found that a
heavy weight placed in the bow of the boat causes it to drift
better. Such a weight in the form of a large stone or anchor,
to which a rope may be attached when let over the side to a
depth of some feet, will prevent the boat drifting too rapidly,
should there happen to be a heavy breeze on.

The boat should always be held broadside on to the wind
to facilitate casting and when a fish is hooked, the boatman
should keep the boat in such a manner that the fish cannot
possibly get underneath it. One can judge from the pull
of the fish and the length and strength of the tackle whether
the man at the oars should or should not follow the fish should
it make a long run for freedom. It is not altogether an easy
matter to handle a landing-net or gaff. If a fish be of a good

size, the boatman should not put the net near it until obtaining instructions to do so.   It is always best to gaff your own fish, and when doing so, the boatman should hold your rod; but if the boatman should gaff the fish, he should go to the far end of the boat from yourself and on bringing the fish alongside near him, he will have a fair chance of cleeking it by putting the gaff over the fish, till the point is in a line with its broadside and then with a strong jerk sink the prong into the beast and lift it over the gunwale as quickly as possible, when the fish should be killed as soon as it is hauled on board, to prevent any unnecessary suffering.

Due consideration should always be paid to the boatman's wants at lunch-time and should a stiff breeze be blowing, nothing is lost by landing at mid-day for a half-hour's rest and a smoke.

Anyone fishing from a boat should take care not to drift too close to any other boat which might happen to be fishing the same loch and anyone intending to drift a bay already in possession of another angler, should take up a position a good way behind or at the outside of, and in line with the latter; but at such a distance as not to interfere with the boat already in possession of the drift.   A fly fisher should be allowed the first ground in preference to anyone using trolling tackle.

On fishing from the same boat with a friend, one should confine oneself strictly to one's own share of the water; but if you have a boat to yourself, it is advisable to stand as near the centre of it as possible, without interfering with the boatman in rowing and cover as much water in front of you and as far to the sides as the breeze will permit.   The flies should land lightly on the water, as rises cannot be expected if any undue splash is made.   After casting, the line should be slowly drawn towards the boat by raising the point of the rod and care should be taken to keep the line as taut as possible with the bob fly upon the surface.   Casting of long lines should be avoided unless you see a feeding fish rise a good way ahead.   Casting should be frequent as the most deadly time is when the flies actually touch the water.   While on good fishing ground, one should never stop casting, as one never knows the moment a good fish may rise, and it is imperative to keep one's eyes on the flies and not to let one's attention be distracted so long as the flies are in the water, in order that striking may be carried out *de rigor*. It is an old theory, but an accurate one, that on a clear day, flies of sombre hue should be used; but brighter flies should be tried on a dark day, the size being regulated according to the breeze. One should always err on the side of small flies and, when a fish rises, one should strike immediately. By the time the angler sees the fish lunge at his flies, he may conclude that the fish has already seized or missed one of them, and the sooner he ascertains the true state of affairs by striking instantaneously, the better; but in striking, the least tightening of the line is sufficient, and this is usually performed by a turn of the wrist.

There is no doubt that, in loch fishing, one has ample scope to enjoy the grand scenery and the fresh air. There are four outstanding species of loch fish in our Scottish waters: (1) *Salmo fario*; (2) *Salmo trutta*; (3) *Salmo salar* (usually termed " fish "); and (4) *Salmo ferox*. The last-named rarely rises to the fly.

When a fish is hooked, no time should be wasted in bringing it to the net or the gaff and, when playing a fish, the line should never be allowed to get slack unless when he leaps into the air—then he must be given plenty rope. A fish should always be played windward of the boat, especially if there is someone sharing it with you. This allows him to continue casting to leeward. Once an angler finds confidence in the strength of his tackle, he will soon learn to judge the proper strain to put on it; but, generally, some care and considerable play are necessary.

For its size, without a doubt, the gamest fish of all is the sea trout which generally fights harder for his life than a salmon twice its size. It gives one a grand thrill to see a good sea trout rise with no half-hearted attempt and it leaves you the tiniest part of a moment to strike. In my opinion fishing for sea trout with the fly is the most exciting form of sport one could possibly wish for. For salmon, the tackle used is proportionately heavy and, after the fish is hooked, with the exception of the first few mad rushes, there is little in it, except a matter of time. The chances are that a hungry fish will not miss the lure and so the charm generally of salmon fishing is in the rising and in the striking. The strike should not be made too soon and should not be attempted until the fish has broken the surface of the water. The strike should be a determined stroke, not a mere tightening of the line as in trout fishing. I have never known a salmon fisher who did not enjoy trout fishing every bit as much in its own way.

Salmo ferox usually possess features distinct from the ordinary loch trout and, when hooked, show a remarkable amount of fight, not to be equalled by any of his neighbours. A large *ferox* will render a great deal of amusement and excitement for an indefinite time and will battle to the finish. In fact, the angler is never sure of him until he is in the boat; but days may be spent trolling for *ferox* without even getting a run.

The great secret of loch fishing is not to be discouraged. Keep on casting and try to keep the flies in the water as much as possible.

After a hot bath on coming off the loch at the conclusion of a fatiguing day with the rod, the angler always enjoys a good dinner and a good refreshment. Dinner over, he should turn his attention to the tackle in preparation for the next day's outing. Lines should be dried by means of winding them round the backs of chairs and reels and rods and casting lines and traces overhauled. Gut should be left soaking in saucers of water overnight.

The man who lives to a ripe old age without having been a keen angler has not only deprived himself of many enjoyments during his life but has neglected to lay up a store for the time when his memory of days on the loch would have made life's closing scenes sweeter.

Sann aig ceann an latha a dh'innsear an sgeul
The fisherman narrates his tale at the end of his day's fishing

CHAPTER V

ANGLING FOR SEA TROUT
IN THE HIGHLANDS

by R. MACDONALD ROBERTSON

THERE is no finer thrill than a battle with a good sea trout. The sea trout (*Salmo-trutta*—family *Salmonidae*) known as Sewen, fights in proportion to its weight and, when fresh-run, its strength is considerably greater than that of a brown trout of same size. Sea trout being homeless vagrants (visitors to the river) rush madly about when hooked, without selecting any known place of refuge. I would rather accept indifferent sport in a river or burn than fish one of the finest lochs of our Highlands, and I contend that there is no sport to be compared with rambling along the banks of some beautiful Highland stream with rod in hand, where the practiced eye weighs up the possibilities of every part of each successive pool or run. In loch fishing, where a boat is provided, the thrill does not exist to the same extent, as the work entailed is, to say the least, commonplace and more simple than that of exhausting the bed of some rough and rocky mountain stream. The habits of sea trout are similar to those of the salmon in many respects, except that when a salmon is landed, its stomach is usually found to be empty, whereas sea trout feed freely on all sorts of flies and larvae, etc. Sea trout have a keener and quicker sense of perception than salmon or brown trout; but on the other hand, they possess a more natural suspicion or wariness. As spawning approaches a great deal of the shapely brilliance of the fresh-run sea trout is lost.

The Greyling (*Thymallus vulgaris*—family *Salmonidae*) a fresh-water member of the salmon and sea trout species, frequent swift running streams with plenty of water and stony rock bottom.

A sea trout will usually seize the fly under water by making a wild rush at it, so violent that it literally hooks itself and, in view of this, hard striking should be avoided. From the instant a sea trout feels the penetration of the hook, it is on its way to escape and momentarily goes off like mad with a sense of resentment coupled with rage; but, after a stay of any length in fresh water, sea trout get sluggish and disinclined to move, and although they take better after a flood, they rarely come to the fly with the same dash as when they were newly up from the sea. There is no more exciting sight than a silver beauty threshing the surface of the water into foam after tearing foot after foot of the line from the reel.

When rivers run high and the stream is strong, it is advisable to exhaust the smoother currents at the tail of deep pools, but strict attention should be paid to rushes at heads of shallow rippling flats. If the river is in normal condition, the only guide to the best places to fish is by constantly casting from pool to pool. When the river is low, provided sea trout are running, they usually collect in pools and take during a breeze which ruffles the surface.

The violent antics of the sea trout, when first hooked, are certainly in a degree more spectacular and faster than those displayed by an ordinary brown trout of equal weight; but actually the sea trout comes to net in less time than the " brownie ", owing to the fearful energy which it expends in fight, especially if it exhausts itself by leaping out of the water —a characteristic of the species—when held firmly by the hook and extra strain put upon the line, immediately results in the fish giving a mighty jump for freedom. A quiet backwater with a shelving gravel ledge is an ideal place in which to find and land a sea trout.

Sea trout as a rule will take similar baits to those presented to salmon and brown trout, and should the water be suitable for fly-fishing, a hook dressed with a silver body and a little red tag, will generally prove most deadly.

There is a weird fascination in night-time fishing. The

silence is often broken by the unexpected splash of some feeding fish near the reeds, the bark of the deer or the night-birds' cry.   The angler can fish in the darkness with coarser and stronger tackle and cast a shorter line than he would do during the day time.

It is wrong to imagine that it is useless to fish for sea trout among the froth which lines the surface of a rocky pool when the burn is in flood, for what the angler sees from dry land, the trout don't—or more correctly—the fisher cannot perceive all that the trout see (or smell) from below.

In baiting, the hook should be covered, leaving the barb to project through the tail so that the worm can wriggle naturally.

During heavy spates, fish are generally caught close in to the bank, where the current is less strong, as they take shelter in the eddies in the quieter sides of the stream.   In Autumn, when rivers are in good condition as the result of a series of floods, worm will always prove a good lure for sea trout in the upper and middle reaches of most rivers.

So far as fly fishing is concerned, the following sea trout flies, ranging from a small loch trout size to that of a grilse fly, are recommended: Dunkeld, Malloch's Favourite, Blue and Black, Teal and Silver, Mallard and Claret, Silver Doctor, Greenwell's Glory and Alexandra Glory.   When other flies fail, a Blue Charm should be tried, especially in the late evening. If the water is in condition, my experience has been that this fly may not only raise a sea trout but perhaps a salmon or grilse as well; but fish rather slower in the dusk and keep the bob fly on the surface of the water.

It is always a safe precaution to use single fly hooks in preference to the double kind, as with the latter the barbs tend to give leverage against each other's hold, in consequence of which they are apt to become torn out more easily than the single hook.   In any event, too small a size of hook is apt to tear its way out of the mouth of a large fish and the mouth of a freshly run sea trout is usually very tender.

Sea trout are distinctly more nocturnal in their habits than salmon.   By using small flies during twilight, sea trout are usually to be lured from the lower pools of rivers. For night fishing, flies of the moth variety dressed on Limerick hooks are best; but, if the water be coloured, the angler should use worm—large black-headed kind.

In bait fishing for sea trout, everything which causes the line to halt in its course, be it weed or stone, should be treated as though it were a fish, to enable the angler to have every possible chance of striking one firmly when it does take the bait, for usually when the hook has touched the fish, the sea trout is on its way to escape.

When rivers are in good condition as the result of a succession of floods, the heaviest fish are usually to be found in water most remote from the sea.

In loch fishing especially, it is an important matter to study the wind, for sea trout generally lie along the shore on which there is a breeze and, if the wind is blowing hard, they usually lie close inshore. When angling for sea trout in salt water, it is essential to study the tides, as the best times are roughly two hours before and two hours after low water, if the sea trout happen to be on the move out, and twice daily when one is dealing with incoming fish that have no reason to suspect the angler.

I have frequently observed sea trout circling in shoals round the mouths of rivers, but refraining from entering the fresh water until, on a sudden impulse, the whole pack made their way up-stream with great persistence. In salt water especially, flies without hackle are deadly for sea trout.

The best time to fish tidal waters for sea trout is in the late evening when darkness is falling, an hour or so after the ebb has finished, when a rise usually occurs unless the breeze is adverse and the best method is to cast across the flow of the current off the bar.

Should the angler yearn for thrills, let him hook a strong sea trout of 3 lbs. or over, on a light rod and rather fine tackle and be compelled to play it within uncomfortable proximity to dense and unbreakable reeds. As the fish tears foot after foot from the reel, he will admit that the excitement is quite sufficient for anyone not blessed with cast-iron nerves.

In conclusion, may I venture to say that in my humble opinion it is curiosity which causes the average angler to fish as much as he does.

Breac a linne, slat a coille, is fiadh a fireach, meirle anns nach do ghabh Gaidheal riamh naire

A fish from the river, a wand from the wood and a deer from the forest—three thefts no Gael is ashamed of at any time

CHAPTER VI

THE BRIG O' DUN SALMON

by J. D. WATKINS-PITCHFORD

A FEW YEARS before the war I used to visit Montrose each winter for the wildfowling.

In those days it was a quiet unspoilt locality as the aerodrome had not been completed and many were the good " flights " I enjoyed at the wild geese which then frequented the basin in considerable numbers. Ducks and teal were also plentiful as, when the tide was out, the major part of the basin was uncovered forming the resting and feeding place of all manner of wildfowl. Alas! those days are now a memory but maybe the salmon and finnock still run up the South Esk as they used to do of old, and maybe it is still possible to purchase a half-crown ticket at the Brig o' Dun and enjoy a day after the salmon.

The South Esk, where it flows into the basin, is not a large river, but it is fairly swift and the banks are high. Wading is possible in some places—I am speaking of the water between the Brig o' Dun and the Basin proper—but for the most part one must fish from the bank top.

One September day in 1936 a friend and I, abandoning our guns for once, decided we would motor over from Arbroath, where we were staying for the shooting, and try our luck for some finnock in the Brig o' Dun water.

I started from below the bridge, while Captain Oakey went about a quarter of a mile below me. The day was close and oppressive, cloud covered the sky, yet no rain threatened; it was a typical autumn afternoon. Already spots of yellow were visible in the oaks below the " brig ", the mountain ash trees still showed orange yellow berries but the big mistle thrushes had had most. The gnats were an in-

30

tolerable nuisance. I often think that the gnats of Scotland are the most vicious in the whole of Britain. That afternoon they plagued my life out and I had to keep up a constant winnowing with my left hand while with my right I plied my light trouting rod, a split cane of no particular pedigree.

I caught no sizeable fish, though finnock exasperatingly leapt and gambolled all over the river, for the tide was rising, and I saw a stout lady in waders and mackintosh catch several, one after the other. But nothing came to me but " smouts ".

It was evident that something was amiss and that my tactics were wrong. Lighting a pipe and feeling very disgruntled I flung myself down on the grassy bank and sourly watched the stout lady secure two more finnock in quick succession.

Below me the river ran swift and deep into the neck of a fair-sized pool. Now and again a finnock leapt up to mock me and fell back with a loud splash. I smoked on and wondered how my friend the Captain was faring farther down.

The stout lady now came out of the river where she had been fishing a lower pool and, with groaning basket, she came back past me, along the top of the bank. " Have you had an offer? " she asked me. She had a deep voice like a man's, and an Eton crop. When I told her " no " she displayed to me her basket. She had caught many fat finnock.

I smoked on and soon fell into a reverie of past tramps along this very bank on my way to morning flight. I heard again the exciting clang of geese and saw the skeins rising from the muds and heading out inland.

Splunge! A mighty disturbance broke my thoughts. Some fish, obviously a salmon, had jumped in the pool directly below me. I sat up and stared at the sherry coloured ripples which were deepening every moment with the incoming tide.

As I looked a miraculous vision appeared. A vast silver torpedo, shot with metallic lights and colours, again hoisted itself suddenly out of the pool, gave a sideways jerk as it hurtled through the air, and fell back with resounding splash. What a fish! I put him at over twenty pounds, nearer thirty, clean run, with the sea lice on him!

Feverishly I changed my tackle, putting on a heavy line and a salmon cast. And then I found I had no salmon fly in my book. I had not thought of salmon. All I had was a large fly not unlike an outsize Silver Doctor. I had purchased that fly in Austria when I was fishing that wonderful trout river—perhaps the best in Europe—the Traun. I had purchased it on the advice of my *fischer* and it had been designed to bring about the downfall, or perhaps it would be better to say " uphaul ", of a truly fantastic trout which the *fischer* assured me weighed ten kilos (over twenty pounds).

This monstrous creature was to be seen every day lurking below some piles near the Gmunden Weirs but he never looked at my fly and I will wager that he would never be caught by such a lure. A minnow was more to his taste and spinning was forbidden on the Traun. However, perhaps this gaudy fly might at last justify itself, thought I, as I tied it to my cast. But my little rod was no match for such a fish, it would take two days to kill a salmon with such a trivial weapon.

" You'll no' catch yon fush! "

" Eh, what's that? " said I, looking up.

" I said, you'll no' catch yon fush while he's jumping. I've been over him most of the morning and he won't look at me."

My informant, a " local " evidently, gave another hitch to the rod on his shoulder and passed on up towards the Brig o' Dun. Old beast, I thought, I jolly well *will* catch this salmon just to spite you! I hate those croaking pessimists who come along and wish you no success.

I began to cast over the brown water. At my second cast that wondrous salmon rose again, clean cut, within six inches of my fly. As he fell back into the arms of the river, his round urgent eyes seemed to be staring into mine with complete astonishment, an expression which was mutual.

I cast again and was just drawing in my fly when the rod was nearly wrenched from my hands. For a second I could not imagine what had happened. I had never hooked a salmon before. The white bone handle of my reel was a blur, the reel itself screamed as if in pain.

PLATE IV

Detecting a " rise " on a Highland Loch

Then that huge fish charged right across the river and the next second was lying high and dry on the opposite shingle! I did not know what to do, I was quite unversed in the ways of salmon. There lay the fish waiting to be picked up! At least that was what passed through my mind. But in a moment he gave a mighty fillip and was back into the river and the reel screamed anew. He ran out forty yards of line and was soon on to the backing. He was travelling still, straight for the sea. I was down at the foot of the bank. I could not follow along the edge. Could I leap for the bank top and race with him? But it was not to be. As I turned with anxious face and (I must confess) trembling arm, to scramble up, the reel fell silent, its scream stopped as a pig's squeal is stopped by the butcher's murderous knife. Sorrowfully I reeled in. Something was amiss. There was no real reason why that line should have parted like that.

Almost weeping with disappoinmtent I examined the reel and soon the cause was clearly evident. The fish had run out the backing until he had come to a tangle. The line had been carelessly wound upon the drum of the reel—I had never dreamt that any fish I hooked would ever demand such a length of line!—and that was why I lost my first salmon.

Lots of people have written of how they caught their first salmon—well—I have written, unashamedly, of how I *lost* my first!

D

RETURN OF THE SALMON

Look how they come, the silvery ones,
Survivors of the migrant school,
Which forsook birth-place to obey
The restless urge and steady pull
Of Nature and the sea.

O! How they speed, racing the tide,
Until, at last, they bid farewell
To pastures salt, which gave them strength;
A driving impulse does compel
The exiles to seek home.

See how they surge, leaping with joy
At each fresh touch of water pure,
They work against the currents strong,
And thrust and flash with instinct sure
Towards their natal ground.

They pause for rest in pool and eddy,
Nosing out each sheltered lie,
Then play awhile, by jumps and swirls
And stately rolls, with tails on high,
They demonstrate their glee.

Gamely they face each set-back dire,
Hazarding all, that they may keep
Their tryst with Time, and thus create
New Life, for Nature's purpose deep;
The dauntless Silver Host.

IAN ARMSTRONG

CHAPTER VII

DO SALMON FEED IN FRESH WATER?

by R. MACDONALD ROBERTSON

Some people regard fish as either salt water or fresh water creatures. The salmon (*salmo salar*) species belong to both these categories being, according to the season, found in the sea and in fresh water.

The general theory is that such fish which migrate from the salt water to the fresh, do so not in search of food but for breeding purposes, and to undertake their purpose they make most stupendous journeys in order to find a suitable nursery for their offspring. Fasting is a sexual accompaniment to the journey.

In this formidable journey up stream, thousands never reach their destination, some falling to the angler's rod, while still more are captured by nets spread around the coast or placed across rivers. Only a small percentage of salmon escape the ingenuity of mankind; but those that do, have frequently to encounter such obstacles as waterfalls.

Again and again the salmon faces foaming waters, leaping up falls from rock to rock with fierce determined rushes, battling upwards, resting but a moment until the final height is mastered, and many fall back exhausted in their attempt.* Still the desire to reach their objective is so strong that they keep on trying until finally their efforts are usually crowned with success. Falls and weirs do not deter the salmon. So long as there are points in the ascent not more than approximately six feet apart, he will get up leap by leap. Of course, salmon do at times make mistakes by jumping out on to the bank or into a boat! Some years ago I helped a salmon, which had jumped right on to the rocky bank below the Falls of Shin,

* The salmon—" the leaper "—from *salire*, to leap is fitly named.

Sutherland, back into the pool below. Had it not been Sunday, I might have acted differently!

After overcoming their obstacles, salmon lie exhausted for some time to rest, but before they attain their object, much remains to be accomplished, for the males battle fiercely with each other for the possession of the female, and to such a pitch that one or other of the combatants succumbs. The lower jaw of the male grows and grows until a formidable hook-like projection is established in front, not due to the effect of fresh water but to the urgent hand of nature which causes the transformation. The fierce seeming beak is not a weapon of offence (not bone but cartilage—therefore not so deadly as it seems) but the marvellous provision to prevent males from exterminating themselves wholesale when they battle furiously for their mates. Conflicts and murders are the normal sequence of events which lead fish to their brides in our inland waters to fertilise the eggs laid by the female, before returning, lean and lanky, to the sea whence they came.

Brevetatis causa, the process of spawning can be described as follows:

Male and female fish of about equal size, working upstream, select a gravelly shallow in the river where the current is not too strong and commence digging a trench some inches deep across the stream. Both co-operate in making the spawning-bed and cover it as soon as the eggs are laid. The female rolls on her side, and by flapping her tail, fans up the sand. The action of the combined tails and fins of both fishes buries the eggs as soon as they are impregnated. On depositing her ova, commencing at the lower end of the trough, or hollow, the female leaves the " Redd " (a place made ready or prepared) and the male then moves up and sheds his milt on her spawn. When both have performed their share of the work, they make a parallel trough immediately above the former one and cover up the spawn in the first trench with the sand and gravel from the second. The process is repeated until all the spawn is exhausted and then the fish return to the salt water. Salmon have been known to breed with large river brown trout; likewise brown trout with sea trout. *Ob majorem cautelem*, the ova is always covered, nature protecting herself from the ravages of gulls and other birds above and from trout and eels below.

The strenuous months the salmon have spent in fresh water strangely transform them, their silvery sheen having disappeared.

Year after year, salmon return to the place of their birth.

All fish are cold blooded and nearly insensible to pain, their blood being only two degrees warmer than the element in which they live. The senses of sight, taste and hearing are, however, well developed, and particularly smell, which chiefly guides the salmon to its old haunts. So far as hearing is concerned, fish keenly sense vibration, water being an excellent conductor of sound. It conveys noise of any kind a great distance—nearly as quickly as air.

The growth of fish corresponds to their power of eating and many species have a very rapid rate of digestion.

Fish yield their eggs by thousands of millions according to the danger incurred in the progress of their growth. There is no other creature in the animal world that can, in this respect, be compared to them, except perhaps the queen bee or the white ant, or that terrible domestic parasite to which no one cares to make reference!

The Pacific salmon differs from the Atlantic salmon in this respect, that it only makes but one journey to the river, and, once spawning has taken place, it dies. In this degree, Pacific salmon resemble the fresh-water eel.

It has been suggested that the salmon fasts throughout the whole of its stay in fresh water. Why therefore, is it so easily captured by rod and line? The salmon fly is commonly like nothing in nature; yet it is greedily seized (whether by way of curiosity or not) likewise the worm and other strange baits such as an eye taken from the carcase of a freshly slaughtered sheep.

With each opening of the spring angling season, the case for and against the theory that salmon do not eat when in fresh water, is resurrected again and again and must still remain not only a mystery, but a sore point to the salmon fisher. At any rate, the experienced angler usually reserves his own opinion on this point; but if still in doubt, let him put the matter to the test and he will usually find that, when the river is rising after heavy rain, by stringing more than one big dew-worm on a large single round-bend bait hook and sinking the wriggling mass deep into a pool in which salmon are in the habit of frequenting, he will not generally be disappointed.

Big fish eat lesser fish, lesser fish eat smaller fish, the smallest eat the water fleas, and their comrades eat the green vegetable life of the stream.

The fry of salmon are called " parrs " until they put on their migratory armour, when they become " smolts " and go down to the sea. " Grilse " (young of salmon on their first return from salt water) if they return from the sea during the first year of their migration, are then classed at all other periods under the category of " salmon ".

There is enough evidence to prove that salmon and grilse find their way back to spawn in the rivers in which they were bred. In fact to the identical spots and return to the sea as " spent fish " or " kelts "—returning during the next four or five months as " clean fish ", and with an increase in weight from some six to ten pounds.

Before spawning (and whilst returning to the sea as " spent fish "), salmon are unfit for food, and their capture is illegal. If males, " foul fish " before spawning, turn orange-red in colour, females are darker in colour and are called " black fish ". After spawning, the males are termed " kippers " and the females are called " baggits ".

When ascending from the sea, salmon are termed " fresh-run ". They are then in the most perfect condition having a bright silver-blue on the stomach and sides. Sea lice are frequently found sticking to the " fresh-run " fish. The fresh water soon kills the sea lice but the salmon retain the scars for some time.

Salmon have been known to eat the sea lice in fresh water. Curiously enough, people to-day dispute the fact of salmon feeding in fresh water; but a specialist, who has been in the habit of opening the salmon he caught, records that he did find pre-digested remains of shrimps, minnows, and parr in the stomach.

Having fished salmon for now well over a quarter of a century, I take the liberty of listing a few of the more uncommon baits, which have, in my experience, worked the oracle with salmon on ordinary bait hooks or Archer-spinners when all other lures (such as natural or artificial minnows) failed, while trolling on fresh-water Highland lochs: goldfish, dead mice, piece of red rubber inner tube of motor car tyre, rubber finger-stole, thumb of old kid-glove, pig's tail, bit of tartan from kilt, small slice of fresh herring or kipper, strip of old school tie, etc. Therefore I have *ipso facto* come to the conclusion that apart from the orthodox salmon flies (or flags of all nations), while in the mood, salmon (like the pike) will " take " almost anything within reason presented to them. Of course, " taking " does not always imply " eating ".

This problem as to whether salmon do or do not eat in fresh water, is a very controversial matter amongst fishers and even amongst scientists and biologists; but I think the view that salmon do *not* feed in fresh water is the one accepted by the vast majority of anglers.

P. D. Malloch in his book on the salmon contends that he has examined thousands of salmon and has never found a trace of food inside any of them. He adds that he has dropped unhooked bait from a bridge and has seen the fish take it and subsequently eject it; but again, other writers contradict this theory. A common belief amongst Highland game-keepers is that on account of the rapid digestion of the salmon, the food passes through their intestines with amazing speed.

In conclusion, a wee bit nibble at the ordinary worm has often landed a salmon gasping on the bank; but as yet, no one has been sufficiently able or enterprising enough to fully solve the problem as to whether salmon do or do not feed in fresh water.

The peculiar and often well-defined line which runs down the middle of the body on both sides of the salmon (and other fish), extending from the head to the tail, is known as the

" Lateral Line " or the " Line of Sensitivity ". This line is
formed by a series of perforations in the scales. These perforations are filled with mucus and are richly supplied with nerves
—an organ for the reception of mechanical stimuli transmitted
through the surrounding water. This sensory organ is repre-
sented in the head by a series of inter-communicating tubes
which open along definite tracts on the surface. Fish not only
sense vibrations through their Lateral Lines, but sight, smell,
taste and memory, as well as other important natural pheno-
mena, including the instinctive provision of divining, which
compels the salmon to return to the same river from whence
they went to sea after being hatched. The skull or cranium
forms the receptacle for the brain and the organs of sight, etc.,
and the brain performs the " Extra Sense " of piloting the
fish back to the land of its birth.

The swallow and other migratory birds also possess, somewhat equivalent to the salmon, the same kind of sensitivity of
divinition which enable them to return year after year to the
same place of their birth. There are most unaccountable
instances of the acuteness of the raven's instinct which leads
the bird to the carcase of an animal and often on the near
approach of the animal's death. Long before an approaching
storm, pigs become restless and start to prepare their beds;
mountain sheep seek shelter in the leeside of the hills, while
grouse fly to the dry heights. There are recorded instances of
" Seers " also dogs having proclaimed deaths of human beings
hours before they have eventuated and many a " Dowser "
has been able to locate a body on the lonely hillside by the
aid of a " Divining Rod " (a V-shaped twig of hazel); but
perhaps fish possess the strongest instinct of all creatures with
regard to changes of weather and other conditions.

Sceptical persons scoff at the scientific reality of prevision;
but others consider that it is no mere superstition—on the
contrary, that it is an actual gift or art which average man has
lost through the ages or allowed to fall into disusage, possibly
brought about on account of the modern rush of everyday
life. Were we to study more closely the everyday instinct
and habits of the animal kingdom, there would be a greater

amount of valuable information to be gleaned, especially in relation to our tender regard for our ancestral waters.

In a certain Highland river, the Laird contends that the salmon seriously injure the trout multitude, as the young of the salmon devour the food of the trout, and that the spawning beds of trout are frequently disturbed by the salmon, the hungry kelts eating the young trout.

There are many instances of salmon " swallowing " a bait in fresh water such as a boiled prawn—a lure such as he has never seen anything like before; and the salmon will often keep the prawn in its mouth for some time before gorging it.

Nevertheless, I contend that worming for salmon, although a deadly way of taking fish, is an unsportsmanlike method and should be condemned by all clean sportsmen. A bunch of worms threaded on an ordinary large bait hook—granted the lowest form of salmon angling—has often won the day, the hook generally being found fixed in the gullet of the fish; but I think it is perhaps safer to postulate that salmon will " swallow " in fresh water, rather than to argue that they " feed ".

Trout of mature age often become blind and their colour usually becomes darker as the blindness increases. Trout are of the same species as the salmon. Trout have the power of very quickly changing their colour, to enable them to become in harmony with their surroundings. This change of colour is a protective diligence on the part of the fish—through the eye to the brain and from the brain to the pigment cells. Therefore, when a fish becomes blind, he remains permanently dark in colour and in such cases the crystalline lenses of the eyes, similar to cataract in human beings, becomes opaque.

Fish usually hunt by smell rather than by sight when the river comes down in spate.

Often the water becomes so drumly that the fish cannot possibly see the worms and can only find the lure by taste or smell, and on such occasions the fish usually shelter in some quiet backwater out of the force of the current when the flavour of the bait reaches the feeding fish through the medium of the strength of the stream. It is therefore possible that the salmon discovers the worm in muddy water in much the same way as that of the blind trout.

But whatever be its food, judging from the perfect arrangement of the teeth and the tremendous rate at which it increases in bulk, there can be no doubt that the salmon is a most voracious feeder—although the very small amount of food usually found in the stomach has hitherto been a source of difficulty in ascertaining the exact nature. The singularity of this latter circumstance has often been discussed by writers on ichthyology, and it has been suggested, amongst other less probable explanations, that the gastric juice of the fish was so powerful as to dissolve almost instantaneously whatever was subjected to its action—another, and I am inclined to think, more correct hypothesis being that the fish ejects its food on finding itself hooked or netted.

PLATE V

A Waterfall in Glencoe

CHAPTER VIII

GLEN COE

by R. MACDONALD ROBERTSON

" The wail of the spirits was heard on the mountain,
    As cruel as adders, they stung them while sleeping,
But vengeance shall track ye wherever you go,
    Our loved ones lie murdered, no sorrow or weeping
Shall ever awaken the sons of Glencoe."

PRAYER FOR A CROFT IN THE PASS OF GLENCOE

" May nothing evil cross this door
    And all ill-fortune never pry
About these windows may the roar
    And winds go by.

Strengthened by faith, these rafters will
    Withstand the battering of the storm;
This hearth, though all the world go chill,
    Will keep us warm."

IT WAS LATE one Saturday night in August, 1938, when we pulled up at Kingshouse Inn on our way through Glen Coe to Ballachulish and thence to the regions of the far North. As much has already been written concerning the Massacre of Glencoe, I do not intend to dwell on the subject other than to say, that even at the present time the Campbells are condemned in the Glen, for out of two hundred Macdonalds of the Pass, at least forty were slain and many more died from exposure, and more would have perished had not the severity of the weather prevented the Royal Troops reaching the passes in time. Even unto the present day few Macdonalds, if any, will attend divine worship in the Glen if a Campbell occupies

43

the pulpit; but I argue that, after all, we should not condemn a man for original sin!

Glencoe signifies the Glen of weeping; and in truth, that pass, prior to the construction of the new road, was one of the most dreary and melancholy of Scottish passes—the very valley of the shadow of death. " Mists and storms brood over it, through the greater part of the finest summer; and even on those rare days when the sun is bright, and when there is no cloud in the sky, the impression made by the landscape is sad and awful."

Innumerable torrents foam down the rifted rocks to join the main waters of the River Coe, and so it was on the day we set out to fish it!

But the night on which we arrived at Kingshouse Inn, a Ceilidh* was in progress to celebrate a local wedding, and there was excellent pipe music and dancing. All this performance carried on without a halt until the early hours of the morning. Nevertheless, we were all invited to join in the fun and this we certainly did, and the *aqua* flowed like the waterfalls outside.

In the morning we felt very tired as the result of dancing reels the night before, and when a minister sitting at the next table injudiciously lamented the fact that Big Donald " drank like a fish ", we, with all deference, felt it our duty to contradict this somewhat false and unfounded charge, for FISH DO NOT DRINK and we told him so! For the breathing of fishes is entirely contributed to the characteristic movements of the mouth, rarely properly understood by the lay mind. Naturally the rythmical opening and closing of the mouth illustrates " drinking ". This is not so. It is merely the outward sign of the act of breathing which corresponds to " the heaving sides and the steaming nostrils of the galloping horse ".

When a fish opens its mouth, it draws in water; but, in closing it, the water is forced out again through its gill-slits in the gullet. In this way the oxygen is exuded and NO WATER

* An informal gathering of Highland folk where song, recitation, music, gossip and story telling are enjoyed. The Gaelic word for " a musical evening ". The word is used as a noun or a verb for " to ceilidh " means to get together for a thoroughly lively evening in true Highland form.

IS SWALLOWED in the act, because the gills contract themselves so tightly that the entrance of water to the stomach is checked. The contraction is entirely controlled by muscles in the same way as a double string twisted round the mouth of (shall I say) a rubber balloon. When a fish feeds, the muscles relax and the " tit-bits ", presented lightly against the centre of the closed up gullet, are devoured. So perfectly is the swallowing act performed that practically no water is swallowed at all; because the gullet presses round so tightly that the food eaten might easily be compared with a cork being thrust down the neck of a bottle (with a flexible neck) which retracts as the cork is pressed lower and lower down.

When we reached the river with rod in hand, we found the burn bank-high and in angry mood; but we did manage to land a few plump beauties with worm from the calmer waters almost about a foot or so from off the river bank.

As we carried on down stream casting here and there where possible, I remarked to my friend that there was too much water for successful fishing to which he replied: " You never know what will happen when heavy water conditions prevail," but, notwithstanding that the stream was too fierce and too flooded to afford satisfactory results, my friend being an expert, had a very fine basket of brown trout in a few hours.

We lunched in the drenching rain near the main fall on the burn, which is very picturesque. It is not a very high waterfall but a very lovely one—a towering cascade which spurts out from off the hump-backed cliff describing a curve before pouring down in a series of low contracted falls from one dark basin to another. From each side of the swollen stream, impetuous torrents foam downhill to meet the main stream in its headlong rush seaward. The impending gloomy precipices of this wild glen are of a nature to strike the most unreflecting mind with awe; their rugged outlines and bold fronts scarred with torrents and shattered by storms, form a scene not only wonderful but terrific.

After lunch, realising that the fishing would be almost impossible, we decided to explore the waterfall and to take a photograph or two.

With difficulty we made our way across the flooded waters of the stream at a point where the lesser current spreads out over a ragged stretch of shingle.

Reader, have you ever beheld a waterfall from behind it, instead of gazing upon it from the front—so to speak?

To view the waterfall from its wrong side is one of the most fascinating things imaginable—and we did so, by crawling along a narrow ridge of rock which admitted us to close proximity of the crashing waters of the burn where the sheeted volume of the cascade threw an unearthly light over the rocky hollow below the top fall into which cavity we crawled, and over which the water shot out from a perpendicular ridge of cliff above us.

Behind us were corners of dark rock with many a grizzly furrow; but on we pressed, on all fours, determined to explore the majesty of the scene.

This cataract resembles, in a very miniature scale, the top portion of that of " Eas-coul-Aulin " in Sutherland (said to be Scotland's highest waterfall) which, during the long continued rains of open winter, descends in thunder from off the cliff, presenting its broad undulating front of white foam against the dark background of rock.

Foot by foot we crept towards the hollow behind the upper waterfall. It was weird behind the fall as the torrent bursting from overhead, confined by its narrow channel above, shot in one unbroken column, white as snow, into a basin quarter way down the whole extent of the cascade, from which clouds of vapour ascended to the perpetual roar of the falling water. We hung on for dear life to one or two out-jutting corners of rock in a cavity of blue-white light produced from the ever moving film of water hurtling itself downwards before us, which at times had the appearance of a solid thick glass curtain in perpetual motion as it swished into the steaming cauldron below us. We found it difficult to tear our gaze away from that awe-inspiring scene of descending water. It was to us like a dream; but luckily we had sufficient space between the fall and the rocks behind us to give us that sense of security.

By the height and energy of the waterfall, spray was created forming a perpetual shower of glittering dew-drops and innumerable rainbows, casting a gloomy mist over the caverned rocks, rising like the smoke of a furnace into the air. There was something in the semi-darkness and imprisonment of the wild overhanging ledges of rock above—inexpressibly awful, combined with the thundering sound of a dozen echoes.

As we balanced ourselves on the ledge of rock and beheld the mass of tumbling water shooting downwards from above, our feelings were excited to the highest degree, while our clothes were drenched through and through; but, after all, being anglers, we were accustomed to this.

Before making our retreat, we were literally blinded by the sharp spray and so deafened by the dashing and clashing and tumbling and rumbling thunder that on gaining a steady foothold on the bank, we had to count ten before pulling our senses together prior to making our journey homeward.

.   .   .   .

I wonder whether any of my readers has ever heard this somewhat unusual legend of the Glen:

Late one autumn evening an angler was caught in a very severe storm. Soaked to the skin, deafened by thunder and almost blinded by lightning as he battled his way against the elements through this bleak, barren and wind-swept glen, sought refuge at the nearest wayside cottage. Almost exhausted he knocked on the door and begged leave of the crofter to be allowed to shelter for an hour or so until the storm should subside before pursuing his journey.

The crofter, an aged shepherd, welcomed the stranger and led him into his primitive kitchen, where the kettle was hanging from a hook on a chain over a roaring peat fire.

" This storm will not end for hours," said his host, " and if you value your life, you will not attempt to reach Kingshouse to-night as you have several miles to walk. I will be only too pleased to accommodate you here until day-break if you care to partake of my simple hospitality."

The fisherman, who was extremely cold and tired, appreciating the perils entailed in continuing on his way through the night, welcomed the crofter's kindly suggestion and drew his chair into the hearth in order to warm himself and dry his soaking garments.

" My name is Macdonald and I am very glad indeed of your company, sir, on a wild night like this, as I am a very lonely old man, having lived here all by myself since I lost my dear wife some nine years past," said the *bodach*, as he started to prepare a hurried meal. " Tha fios aig Dia agus aig daoine gu bheil còir agam air leòm a bhith orm—is Domhnallach mi! " (" *God and men know that I have a right to be proud—I am a Macdonald!* ").

Just at that moment, while in the act of handing the angler a glass of steaming hot " toddy ", a livid flash of lightning illuminated the semi-darkness, followed by an ear-splitting crash of thunder which almost shook the croft to its foundations, while the rain spat heavily on the tiny window pane.

Over and above the tumult seemed to echo the wailing cry of a child as if in distress, but the stranger, being overwrought, put the matter down to his imagination and made no comment.

During the meal (which consisted of porridge and cream, followed by eggs, potatoes and venison with strong tea) as the storm was at its height, again through the rumble of the thunder came the same mournful cry, followed by the pitiful whine of the shepherd's dog. " Is there someone outside in distress do you think? " said the angler, to which remark the crofter replied: " No sir, there is not a living soul for miles around on a night like this, I can assure you." " Sorry," said the fisherman, " I only imagined I heard a baby crying."

After the meal was over, lamps were lighted round the old-fashioned fireplace when an interesting conversation ensued concerning the district and the history of the ancient Macdonalds of Glen Coe, when Macdonald explained how he hailed from one of the very oldest families of the Glen.

As the wind hissed and whistled through nearly every chink and cranny of the humble dwelling, suddenly burst another loud thunder-clap, which almost rent the rafters and the same weird and plaintive cry of a child somewhere without was overheard above the storm, followed by the bark of the sheep-dog which crouched on a deer-skin rug underneath the kitchen dresser.

" That is a child's cry I hear—the voice of some infant in distress somewhere in the darkness outside," muttered the stranger, " I must go out and rescue the infant."

" You need not trouble yourself," retorted Macdonald, " nothing possible on earth can be done now, for that child has cried at night on the hill-side ever since the Massacre of Glen Coe! "

CHAPTER IX

I RETURN TO THE FINDHORN

by R. MACDONALD ROBERTSON

THE RIVER

"Ah, sweetly the voice of the river is heard, with its deep-toned murmurings, as sweet to me as the voice of a bird, for I love the song it sings. Oh, river, in the days now long gone by, I sat by your gentle stream, and joined my notes to your melody, and told you my youthful dream. The sun shone then as it shines to-day, and the trees were just as fair, but since that day of memory I have known much joy and care. Flow gently, ever pleasant stream, nor time nor change shall age thee, and my real self, whate'er I seem, the same unchanged shall be."

As I have already devoted a chapter to the River Findhorn in the first book I published on the subject of Angling, in 1935, entitled *In Scotland with a Fishing Rod*, I shall try to avoid repetition in the paragraphs which follow, so far as descriptions of this river are concerned.

I had been spending a week's holiday with friends at Forres, who kindly procured for me permission to fish the River Findhorn on the beat immediately below Daltulich Bridge.

It was late September, about the time of the equinox. The frosts had not yet set in and with every breeze came that exhilarating feeling of peaceful satisfaction.

It was a bracing morning when I set out with my host for Daltulich. The sun—bright and red—was presenting a variety of colour through the branches overhead of light and shade when we took the road in a southerly direction. As we gradually ascended in the direction of Regulas, the summits of the bare and barren mountains, already capped with snow, came into view. Branching right of Regulas, we followed up the course of the river until we reached Daltulich Bridge where we drew the car up on a grassy bank by the side of the road.

I can state without hesitation that the Findhorn is my favourite river, not so much on account of its abundance of fish, but for the sport it affords in catching them, owing to the wild and rugged bed through which the waters rush and boil in wild confusion.

Every thicket possessed a rich mixture of russet and emerald green as we wandered through a wooded glade down to the waterside, while the song of the birds overhead blended harmoniously with the roar of the river.

The sportsman who follows the pursuit of salmon, sea trout and brown trout up the rough and dangerous passes lying between the gigantic rocks which overhang the deep black pools and foaming torrents of this river between Dulsie Bridge and this section of the Findhorn, may indeed fall under the category of the acrobat. That is to say, if he conducts his fishing in serious mode with an endeavour to exhaust every nook and cranny of the stream.

Having put our rods together, we selected our respective cast of flies and commenced operations down stream.

With nearly his first cast my friend hooked and landed a plump red spotted trout of over half a pound, while almost simultaneously a heavy sea trout lunged at my tail fly and continued jumping three or four times out of the water, as I brought pressure to bear on the line, glittering like silver in the blaze of the sun, making a hard struggle for freedom. Ultimately the fish dived down to the bottom and my flies getting fixed on some sort of formidable obstacle, I lost my cast deep down in the pool. Actually, I did not care so much for the loss of the fish as I did for the loss of my new cast of flies; but after reconciling myself with a cup of tea from my thermos flask, I affixed a new cast to the end of my line and walked off in disgust down the river for about a quarter of a mile, leaving my companion behind.

For about an hour and a half I fished steadily down

stream without rising a fish when, all of a sudden, my rod bent to the scream of my reel and I realised that I had hooked something powerful! This fish played the same cunning tactics as the former one, and dived to the depths, and once again my line fouled the bottom and I was " stuck " in all senses of the word!

In these days I smoked a pipe, and on the spur of the moment I unconsciously removed it from between my teeth and hurriedly put it into the right-hand pocket of my kilt-jacket.

A few minutes later, while I was in the act of endeavouring to bring my captive to the surface, I was enveloped in a cloud of stifling reek, when my first momentary impression was that some of the river-kelpies had kindled one of the old-time lime kilns on the bank immediately behind me. As I felt my side growing hot I discovered to my dismay that I was on fire, when all the weird stories of the Blasted Heath surged through my brain!

Instinctively, I pitched down my rod and, throwing off my jacket, stamped out the blazing material; but while vigorously extinguishing the flames, my reel made itself known and I found that my rod was being hauled steadily into the swirling stream.

My companion who had by this time arrived on the scene, imagined that I was preparing to jump into the cauldron after my prize.

Inch after inch of line was rushing off my reel as I seized the rod in both hands. Owing to the contour of the land, there was only one alternative left and I took the risk.

I ran down the bank and entered the water at a point some thirty yards distant and waded kilt high to the opposite bank over a gravelly stretch of the river, by which time nearly all the line was exhausted from my reel drum.

On getting safely across, I commenced to wind up my reel until I reached the spot opposite where it had originally become entangled deep down in the water, when I commenced to pull my line in all directions but to no purpose—it was firm and fast. I then waded cautiously into the river until the water was well over my thighs, where I was almost directly above the place where my flies were hitched. Feeling my line with my hand under water, I came upon what seemed to me to be a supple-yielding wand and, to my surprise, I caught sight of a wagging tail and realised, to my horror, that my bob fly was firmly affixed to the stump of a tree, which had been carried down the river during a recent spate and which had become partially embedded in the sand.

As I could not nearly reach my fish without diving for it, I got hold of part of the root and, with difficulty, I managed to haul the whole tree-stump, fish and cast up the pebbly beach and by dropping my collapsible landing net over the wriggling mass of energy, I gripped hold of it through the folds of the mesh, and threw it up the bank in a most undignified manner.

The fish—a grilse, turned my pocket scales at just over 5 lbs.—a fresh-run beauty, for which I had fought hard.

The grilse was well hooked, and it must have been splendid gut to have stood the strain.

After partaking of lunch, we again split company, and I continued my way down the river alone, as my friend desired to thrash out, once again, the stretch of water which we had already covered.

About my third cast, a large salmon took my fly (a small Blue Charm). I was rather dismayed, knowing as I did, that I was merely using sea trout tackle; but, having been hooked, I thought he might as well be killed—if possible, and so the battle commenced by the fish darting right out of the rush in which he was first hooked and going down like a stone to the bottom of a black pool below where I stood. Having only comparatively light tackle, I found that I could not force him to any degree; but, after waiting patiently, I, with a gentle but constant strain on my line, finally gave him a tug that dislodged him from his resting spot. Off he went like mad across the river with nearly the whole of my line out, and the next minute he was boiling the water in the pool below the rock on which I stood. Next moment, the salmon took a sudden dart, shaking his head like a stuck pig in an attempt to rub the hook out of his mouth on the shingle; but, realising that he was well hooked, I kept a tight rein on him and took my chance. Instinctively he changed his tactics as I put pressure on the line and he shot straight upwards, leaping several times out of the water, and thereafter desperately ran across the river causing my reel-drum to scream in my hand, and then made down stream in an almighty rush, hauling out every inch of my line, which necessitated immediate gymnastics on my part, by way of leaping from boulder to rock along the water bank, in order to keep pace with him. Ultimately, the fish headed for a somewhat rapid rush of water in the form of a miniature waterfall full of broken rocks, a place where no slender line, such as I was using, could possibly stand the strain. I realised that if he succeeded in once getting down this fall with the weight of water behind him, nothing on earth would hold him. *Hey presto* this he did, as I halted on a submerged rock, making a stand against his pulling; but again the fish changed its mind and came shooting in almost to my very feet, only to rush right back again in the direction directly opposite to where I stood. Not succeeding in winding in my line rapidly enough, the fish headed straight for the fall, and in spite of all I could do to prevent him, he took it, with the result that my line snapped short of my reel and, before I was able to catch hold of it, I had the sickening misfortune of seeing it drifting away down stream, as the fish descended the river to be lost for evermore with about thirty strands of line clinging to him, plus my sea trout cast hanging from his jaws. But I reconciled myself in the words of Charles St. John: " I scarcely knew whether to be angry or amused," and considering that the former would, under the circumstances, be of no use, I partook of a dram from my flask and ultimately undid my rod. So ended my day's sport on my beloved River Findhorn.

I hope to return to the River again to make up for sad losses in the past, and perhaps next time, I may hook and land something really worthy of narrating.

In future I shall come prepared with tackle suitable to play and land relatives of the muckle monster which I lost.

The third time I hope will be the lucky shot!

I recommend the following casts for this stretch of the River Findhorn:

Blue Charm
Tax Collector } 1 × gut
Yellow Sally   No. 8 hook

and

Blue Silver
Grouse and Claret } 1 × gut
Black Pennel   No. 8 hook

alternatively

Black Pennel } 1 × gut
Silver Blue   Nos. 5 to 7 hooks

or

Bloody Butcher } 1 × gut
Invicta   Nos. 5 to 7 hooks

CHAPTER X

FISH FARMING AND OTHER NOTES

by R. MACDONALD ROBERTSON

MANY rivers and lochs in Scotland which readily lend themselves to hatching possibilities of salmon and trout have not yet been exploited for development in this respect.

Salmon and trout production on a scientific scale could form the basis of valuable food repositories if more hatcheries were established in many parts of the country, and I see no reason why ponds and lochs in and around our rural and urban districts should not be commercialised and put into practical use and stocked with trout, not for sport so much, but with a view to supplementing our national food supply in time of food shortage.

Salmon and Trout Hatcheries

In this connection the introduction of Trout Hatcheries might be seriously considered. This would of course probably entail the temporary closing of ponds to the public in order to prevent poaching.

Salmon fisheries (inland and coastal) could be greatly improved and the stock of fish vastly increased were artificial hatching practised on a much larger scale.

An important factor, however, is that the average river is only capable of supporting the number of fish for which nature has provided feeding, and it would be useless to attempt to increase the number of salmon and trout without likewise increasing the food supply for them. It is not very difficult to increase the food supply for fish in (fresh water) lochs and streams. For example, the carcase of a dead sheep, or grass or broom trimmings, deposited into a lochan, form bacteria on which fish thrive.

On the principle of reclamation and preservation, the course of burns which flow through useless peat-bog land could be dammed up where practicable, so as to increase the area of water in the immediate vicinity and flood the swampy ground and rank herbage in the surrounding land—an excellent practice for increasing insect life on which trout thrive. Aquatic plant and animal life could then be introduced and the water stocked with fish. Lump chalk (in proportion to the volume of the water) could also be introduced in order to neutralise the acidity of the peat water, where this be found necessary.

Large inland loch trout have been known to reach more than 30 lbs. weight and there is no reason why they should not grow even weightier where food is abundant, for evidence has shown that fish when granted safety and permitted good feeding can live upwards of fifty years.

Whether food supply actually influences the dimensions of fish to any great extent has been a debatable subject in the past. Some argue that the amount of natural food has no bearing on the size, while others contend that in certain lochs and rivers which contain the minimum of feeding substance, fish of considerable weight are often caught. Again, even in remote waters—free from pollution—in which there is an abundance of natural food, fish average no size of any consequence. But by periodically re-stocking lochs and streams it has been proved that the change of blood strengthens and increases the condition of fish generally, as continual interbreeding causes a degenerate race of a lesser size of trout.

Colouration is very varied in the brown trout species which frequent our Scottish waters. Trout are capable of changing their colour at will, according to their immediate surroundings and the kind of food they prey upon.

Trout with immense ocellated spots are generally found in clear rapid streams. In pools or lochs with a peaty or muddy bottom, trout are usually of a darker colour and, when confined in caves or holes, they assume an almost uniform blackish colouration. Trout taken from hill burns or mountain tarns are either intensely coloured or often quite black. For example, nearly every brown trout I captured while fishing in the semi-darkness within the second chamber of the Smoo Cave, Sutherland, below the waterfall, was as dark as its sinister surroundings. The colour might quite easily be attributed to feeding in this case, as well as to the darkness.

In natural spawning, there is an immense wastage of ova because salmon generally spawn in fast-running streams where frequently the milt fails to reach and fertilise the ova.

It has been estimated that about half the eggs are not fertilised under natural conditions, as the eggs, which take about three months to hatch, are laid in mid-winter, and consequent losses through ice, flood and drought are very considerable.

Many creatures devour ova, and mortality during pre-feeding stages is often very high.

Parr are well able to fend for themselves; but at the smolt stage many enemies await them when they migrate seawards.

Should the dangers of immaturity be overcome, heavy toll of salmon is taken when they feed in the sea, and it has been estimated that out of every 1,000,000 fry, not more than about 1,000 return to the river (in which they were born) as adult salmon.

In a properly conducted hatchery more than 90 per cent. of the eggs placed in the hatching box should hatch out, and a substantial increase in the stock of fish would result if the quantity of fry could be multiplied on the spawning ground. The fry could be sold for re-stocking purposes elsewhere and would, ere long, compensate the initial expense incurred in constructing the hatchery.

Salmon could be introduced into many more of our Scottish rivers by forming resting pools, etc., and by laddering obstructions where necessary, in the course of our streams, before liberating fry into the upper reaches of the water.

Before stocking, the vessel containing the young fish should be immersed in the loch or river until such time as the water in the container reaches the same temperature as that of the loch or river. Then and not until then, the young fish should be liberated. By this method any shock due to sudden change of temperature will be avoided.

The practice of causing artificial spates on certain of our coastal rivers, in order to induce a fresh run of fish from the sea, is already fairly well known.

It is neither a highly specialised nor costly business to erect and conduct a hatchery, and the sale of the fry, for stocking purposes, should at least compensate the initial expense incurred, within a comparatively short space of time.

The necessary knowledge and experience required for fish-farming is not difficult to gain and the maintenance of a hatchery could be undertaken with the minimum number of specially trained employees.

In past years the development of Inland Fisheries has to a large extent been neglected, and vast sources of food supply have consequently been left untapped. This is to be regretted, as there is a large demand in our big cities for coarse fish such as eels, perch, powan (" fresh-water herring " found only in Loch Lomond and Loch Eck) and pike.

Formerly the considerable demand for coarse fish in our larger cities was supplied entirely from continental sources, which resulted in British money being spent abroad instead of at home.

With a view of testing the possibility of catching coarse fish on a commercial basis, and to contributing as much as possible to the Nation's food supply at this time, the Loch Lomond Angling Improvement Association established and equipped a fishing station on the shores of Loch Lomond and has obtained the services of a specially trained crew of fishermen who are engaged in catching eels, netting powan and trapping perch under the direction of Mr. Gerald F. Baird, F.L.A.S., F.S.I., Secretary of the Association.

Well over 5,600 lbs. of powan and 53 drafts of eels were taken from this loch to the market in a season.

Although the perch trapping is still in its initial experimental stages, the results obtained are, so far, most encouraging and it is hoped that very soon it will be possible to make arrangements to operate from five to six hundred traps in Loch Lomond.

These operations, however, to date, should only be regarded as tapping a very small part of Loch Lomond's store of coarse fish; but indicate the possibility of developing a flourishing little industry in future, for the present output could easily be increased five fold.

This would not only increase a useful home industry, but would greatly benefit the salmon, sea trout and trout stocks in the area in which these operations are conducted, as coarse fish, such as those already referred to, can safely be regarded as natural enemies of the salmon kind.

Powan may not be very well known to the general public, but they are excellent eating and the flavour resembles trout.

Were fish-farming developed on a large scale throughout the country, considerably more tons of salmon and trout could be produced for food on the market annually, at a very reduced cost. Further, the tinning industry might, through time, be developed and conducted on an extensive scale and hold its own against foreign competition.

SPEED OF FISH

For some time I have been interested in the speed of various species of fish, and as the result of research and experiment, I have now formed the theory that perhaps the fastest of all fishes which frequent our British Waters, in proportion to their size, are the ordinary (small) sand eels; which move with high rapidity, like most elongated creatures (such as the shark) by fast undulations, the forward motion being effected by the pressure of their bodies against the water. Relatively shorter fishes propel themselves through the water by powerful side to side movements of the tail. It would appear that fish-like form has resolved itself, as the result of adoption, to the mechanical environment. I am informed that an aquarium official once held in his hand a fish about six inches in length while its head was immersed in water and that, when struggling to free itself, it squirted through its gills a quantity of water which rose to the height of nearly four feet—on the " rocket principle "—thus endeavouring to aid its course through the water. This ejection scheme can also explain the degree of speed with which fish are able to turn, almost immediately, at right angles to the direction which they pursue. These ejections propel the fish forward, and in the event of a hurried halt, the fish merely closes its valves and pectorals at right angles in a form of natural locomotion. Even our smaller trout, on account of their construction, are said to be able to overtake the average speed of our latest underwater craft by approximately twenty knots. Perhaps the most beautifully proportioned and streamlined fish is the much condemned pike which can, according to records, in still water, travel at approximately fifteen miles an hour. Submarine warfare might perhaps in future be considered upon similar (natural) lines, having regard to the construction and dimensions of some of our swift-travelling streamlined fishes.

FISHES' SENSE OF SMELL

From the greedy way in which fish seize the artificial fly, it would appear that they cannot possess any refined sense of smell, or any nervous system corresponding to the nasal one in animals, for no odour is given to water by an artificial lure, or at least none like that of a natural fly.

Nevertheless, it would appear that the main function of the nostrils in fishes is to aid the propulsion of water through the gills for performing the act of respiration; but surely there are some nerves which cause fish life to sense the qualities of the water, or of certain substances dissolved in it, or diffused through it, similar to our sense of smell or taste.

There is ample evidence to prove that fishes are attracted by scented worms or salmon roe, and in old angling books there are many recipes given for attracting fish in like manner. Olfactory nerves in fishes are destined for the same function as these nerves in the mammals, especially having regard to the fact that we can perceive odours when the head is immersed in water. The fly usually touches the water by so very small a surface that the air-bubbles on the fringes of its legs can scarcely affect the water so as to give it any power of communicating smell.

CHAPTER XI

ANGLING FOR PIKE

by R. MACDONALD ROBERTSON

THE PIKE (*Esox lucius*—family *Esocidae*) possesses a mouthful of curved-in teeth, and it is essentially a cannibal in its habits and devours fingerlings of its own kind as well as other fish—a wolf with fins and usually no good citizen in trout waters.

This "Poor Man's Salmon" is to-day considered an unmitigated evil, so vast is the havoc wrought by it among the more valuable species of fish. But strictly speaking, the pike is Nature's agent in the loch, just as her agent on the moors is the hawk, and it is just as much in the interests of sport to kill out the one as the other, because an over-populated loch tends to produce a degenerate class of fish, due to want of some agency to keep down their numbers, the fish usually being small and thin from want of sufficient food to support so many.

Favourite haunts of the pike are deep rivers and still ponds, and when a pike is hungry he will eat anything. Despite his bullying and ferocious ways, this fish is faint-hearted and not nearly so high mettled as the trout. When hooked, he often makes a great fuss, throwing himself out of the water, but in the end, dashes to his hold among the weeds. He should be humoured during his mad rush and allowed as much line as possible. He should not be hauled out "instanter" or his escape is inevitable. The time may be calculated in minutes when he grows sick of the conflict.

Young pike are called Jack, and a Jack is termed such until he is approximately 2 lbs. in weight, and a pike when heavier. One of the best lures is a dead minnow of medium size and bright colour, baited on two-hook tackle with gimp substituted for gut. Gimp is stronger than gut and the pike, when hungry, is not easily scared.

According to Charles St. John:

> The principal thing to be regretted in almost all Highland lakes is that there are far too many trout in them, and that the fly-fisher may work for a month without killing a trout of two pounds weight. Pike keep down this overstock, and yet still leave plenty of trout which are of a better size and quality than where they are not thinned . . . A great part of the food of a pike consists of frogs, leeches, weed, etc. Young wild ducks, water-hens, coots and even young rats, do not come amiss to him. Like a shark, when hungry, the pike swallows anything and everything which comes within reach of his murderous jaws.

Personally, I would back a *salmo-ferox* to kill more trout in a day than a pike of the same size would do in a week. I have never landed a tolerably large trout without finding within him the remains of other trout, sometimes too, of a size which must have cost him some trouble to swallow. I would sooner fish where there were pike and catch what I have the skill to land, even be it one good trout, than waste time over the small ones.

Trout are every bit as hungry as pike though not so fearsome. Trout are known to have attempted to swallow young adders and devour mice whole.

Perhaps the best trolling lure for pike is an ordinary piece of raw ox liver tied to the tackle, at the tail of which is secured a small red tassel. As a matter of fact, one can select just about as many baits for pike as there are flies for salmon.

Large pike invariably leave the deep water when on the feed, and make for the shallows.

Pike are by no means piscavorous; they are, to a certain degree, fastidious about their food, inasmuch that the food is preferred alive and not too large to be swallowed. Apart from this, they will attack and devour almost anything; but young fish of any species, including its own, are its great delicacies. In fact, nearly everything that swims, with the exception of salmon and sea trout, etc., in loch, river or canal, is fair quarry. Frogs, waterfowl (especially nestlings) and even rats, mice, newts and shrimps fall victim to this " Freshwater Shark ". Frogs, the pike usually hunts in shallow water, and consumes large numbers of them at a time. According to records, pike are known to have devoured eels up to 2 lbs. in weight.

The only satisfactory method of ridding a loch of the lusty pike is to net it, unless one goes to the trouble of draining it.

The snaring of animals differs from the snaring of fishes, in that in the former case the victim usually enters the snare, while with fish, the snare usually approaches the victim. On account of their shape the pike yield themselves to the wire-noose and the task of wiring the pike is really not difficult. If the wire noose comes gently down stream over the head and past the gills, the pike is easily captured while it rests in the current, head upstream.

Snap-trolling for pike is one of the easiest and deadliest methods of exterminating their species. Drop the bait quietly into the water and lower the tip of the rod. Before the bait has had time to reach the bottom, head first, check it, and draw it slowly in to about three feet, then let it go again. Such an erratic movement is an attraction to pike, which freely seize the lure. Striking should be instantaneous, as a pike generally seizes the bait in its course to the bottom.

Sharp, curved teeth bristle in the pike's mouth, which can inflict ugly wounds, in consequence the angler must use great caution in extracting the hook. He should always kill the fish before doing so in case the pike seizes his hand and lacerates it.

The following angling methods for pike are recommended:

(1) Live-baiting with small fish or frogs, or by trolling with natural bait or spoon-bait or by spinning.

(2) Spoon-bait. The flash of a spoon-bait is frequently more attractive than the rapid spin of an artificial minnow, although natural baits are probably more deadly, as the fish actually smells the lure.

When trolling for pike, wire traces should preferably be used. Frequently pike feed in moonlight during frosty weather, and in the daytime are completely off their feed.

Nearly all the heavy fish I have caught have been with my old-fashioned fourteen-foot rod and a heavy line; but now-a-days anglers prefer to use "threadline" with a breaking strain of four to six pounds, and a short and slender rod. To spin with such tackle is a tricky business, but it is a pleasure to watch a really good angler casting with delicate accuracy, and when the fish is hooked, the playing of it becomes a fine art, using one's wits against those of a game fish.

In olden times, there was a unique sport indulged in and greatly enjoyed by the Earls of Menteith and visitors to the Lake, viz., angling for pike with geese. This singular and curious method of fishing is said to have afforded great amusement. A number of geese were released on the lake, each having a length of line with baited hook tied to one of their legs.

When let loose, the voracious pike would dart upon the lure, and then a grand tug-of-war would commence. If an extra heavy fish got hooked, it would drag the struggling goose below the surface of the water; but the bird would soon reappear and flap its strong wings in an attempt to fly, but would often be dragged beneath again and again, until the web-footed champion would finally land its captive, in triumph, on the bank.

The Lake of Menteith in days of yore was noted for its Daoineshi-water Kelpies, etc., and no doubt the heavy pike which at one time inhabited the depths of this lake, contributed, to a large extent, to the folk-lore of this district.

Reverting to the old-fashioned methods of angling, the following story may interest readers:

A large pike was caught shortly after it had swallowed an empty split-beer-bottle, which the angler, a minute or so before, had thrown over the side of the boat, after consuming the contents. The glinting of the empty bottle in the bright sunlight which prevailed at the time, as it zig-zagged its way down into the depths of the loch, must have resembled the movements of a sick trout (or other fish) and whetted the appetite of the larger denizen of the deep.

From all accounts, it would appear that Sutherland is the only County in Scotland to-day, whose waters are free from pike.

PLATE VI

Two Salmon from Loch Garbet Mor, Kinlochbervie, Sutherland

CHAPTER XII

TROUT FISHING IN THE SOUTH OF THE ISLAND OF SOUTH UIST

by SIDNEY SCOTT, C.B.E.

ODE TO THE HEBRIDES

" Bleak, bare upland and sombre moorland,
Frowning cliffs by a grim cold sea,
Dark still lochs where grey mists gather,
Island of sadness and mystery!

Bright green machair and purple heather,
Glad brown burns that sing to the sea,
Sands agleam in the brave bright weather;
Islands of laughter and witchery!

Islands of mood, matured to our spirit,
Now brooding—now bright like the restless sea,
Near in thy sadness and dear in thy gladness
Ever thy children are thralled to thee."

THE LOCHS of South Uist that are fished from the
Lochboisdale and Carnan Hotels are well known to
many anglers and their manifold attractions have been
chronicled in numerous articles published in fishing books
and periodicals. I have not, however, so far as I can recall,
seen any accounts of the Lochs lying in the south end of the
Island and I am therefore tempted to jot down some of their
characteristics.

These southern Lochs may be fished from Polochar Inn
—a hostelry about six miles from Lochboisdale Pier that has
lately been enlarged and renovated and can now boast of
six or seven bedrooms and a good water supply. The Inn

F   65

has a charming situation on the Sound of Eriskay and commands a fine view of the Islands of Eriskay and Barra and of
the many interesting small isles in the Sound of Barra.   One
can throw a stone into the sea from the door of the hotel.   To
the westward extend miles of firm white sands frequented by
flocks of ringed plover, redshanks and many other varieties
of birds, while to the east is a pleasant path by a rocky shore
interspersed with sandy bays.   A commodious motor-boat
runs between Polochar and Eriskay with His Majesty's Mails
and this can be hired for trips to the adjacent isles.   At any
rate, such was the case when I last visited South Uist.
Therefore on days not suitable for angling, the fisherman can
well fill in his time in pleasant explorations.   And there is
always the main road to Lochboisdale.

A trip to Eriskay is much to be recommended.   There are
practically no roads in the Island, but a stroll over its low
hills, commanding magnificent views of Barra, Uist, etc., is
an unforgettable memory.   As every school-boy knows, Prince
Charlie, in his attempt to regain the kingdom of the Stuarts,
landed first on Eriskay and spent the night on shore there.
The cove where he landed is still called the " Prince's Bay ".
On this cove there grows a somewhat rare spieces of Convolvulus, the seeds of which, local tradition asserts, were sown by
Prince Charlie himself.   To this day the inhabitants of
Eriskay call the flower of this convolvulus " Prince Charlie's
flower ", but nevertheless, it is a little difficult to accept the
supposition that Prince Charlie brought with him from France
a pocket-full of convolvulus seed and that he would find time
or inclination to sow them when his mind was as largely
occupied with plans for regaining the throne of his fathers.

The waters that can be fished from Polochar Inn are, with
the exception of Loch Dunakillie, somewhat small in size, but
they all contain a good stock of brown trout.   For the benefit
of anglers who may not be familiar with them, the following
is a brief review of their characters.

Loch Dunakillie

This Loch is two and a half miles from Polochar and,

being close to the main road to Lochboisdale, can be reached easily either on foot or by car. It is roughly about one mile in length and half-a-mile in width. The Hotel proprietor has a boat on the loch, and a ghillie is generally available. It holds trout of good size and quality, the average weight being three-quarters of a pound. The fish are certainly " dour " and do not rise freely, but they are well worth working for, and are fine fighters, well marked, of pink flesh and excellent flavour. My baskets have ranged from " nil " to eighteen fish weighing 14 lbs., but on a fair day one may generally reckon on landing eight to ten good fish on fly. The Loch is very weedy in parts but, judging from the condition of the fish, affords excellent feeding. I have found dark-coloured flies the most effective and, after having tried many patterns, I consider that a cast with a Black Zulu on the bob, a Grouse and Claret mid way, and a Worm fly on the tail, to be the most deadly. On such a cast I landed the eighteen trout above mentioned. The heaviest fish I have killed myself was one of $2\frac{1}{2}$ lbs. but the proprietor of the Inn assures me that fish of 3 lbs. and upwards are occasionally landed.

Many of the South Uist Lochs are unattractive in their surroundings, but Dunakillie commands a good view of the high lands to the East and can also boast of three green islets. On these islets the Royal Fern grows freely and in the spring one is practically sure of finding a few wild-ducks' nests with eggs. The finest fishing is around these islets and the best months are May, June and July. On the islet at the north end of the Loch are the remains of an ancient " Dun " and from it runs a causeway, now broken down and generally submerged, which at one time connected with the mainland. It is from this " Dun " that the loch takes its name.

Loch Ghaerraidh

This Loch is a long narrow sheet of water lying a little to the westward of Dunakillie and only a few minutes walk distant. It contains trout averaging about half-a-pound, but at certain times of the year is difficult to fish owing to the heavy growth of weed round the shores. At other times it yields good sport.

LOCH AN EILEIN, LOCH CAPULL, LOCH SMERELLET AND LOCH AISOVAT

These waters, with the exception of Aisovat, lie in the extreme south-west corner of the Island. The trout they hold are numerous but small—about three to the pound with an occasional half-pounder. There is no boat available, but they can be easily fished from the shore. Loch Aisovat is about half a mile from Polochar on the east side of the Lochboisdale road. Here again, the fish run about three to the pound but, given a good breeze, large baskets can frequently be obtained. Waders are, however, desirable, as the water close to the shore is shallow.

LOCH KILBRIDE AND LOCH-A-CHOIRE

Good sport can generally be obtained on these Lochs. They are about three quarters of a mile to the east of Polochar Inn and are easily reached by a good road. There is, or was, a boat on Loch-a-Choire and baskets of twenty trout, or more, averaging 6 ounces, can be obtained. Here again, dark coloured flies are most successful.

Three other very interesting small lochs are in the unfrequented South-East corner of the Island, viz., Loch Kearsimal, Loch Marulaig and Loch Moreef. These lochs are rarely fished, with the result that they are overcrowded with small fry. Large baskets (in number) can easily be obtained, but it is hardly likely that the weight of the fish will improve unless the Lochs are netted or more frequently fished. They are, moreover, somewhat difficult of access. The easiest way is to motor to South Lochboisdale and then walk two or three miles over rough country. Moreef can, however, be readily reached by boat from Polochar. A few sea trout find their way up the burn that connects Loch Moreef with the sea and may generally be caught in July and August. The fishing at Moreef will afford much gratification to the angler who loves lonely places where the silence is only accentuated by the call of birds or the occasional bleating of a sheep. No human habitation is near. On an island in Moreef I have found the nests of the Black and the Red Throated Diver. These interesting birds always build their nests very close to the water's edge, their power of locomotion on land being very limited and in great contrast to their speedy movement in the air or in the water. The nests I have met with have usually contained two eggs, dark brown in colour with black spots.

For a quiet holiday, with excellent fishing on Loch Dunakillie, and good baskets of moderate sized fish on the many other lochs, I have no hesitation in recommending Polochar. An additional attraction is the fact that South Uist escapes much of the rain that falls so heavily on the West Coast of the Scottish mainland.

CHAPTER XIII

LOCH MAREE

by HILDA J. C. DONALD

T<small>O MANY</small> anglers Loch Maree is the most beautiful loch in Scotland; its very stones to them are dear. Succeeding generations have fallen under its spell, returning year after year to fish its broad waters.

The setting of the Loch is unique; massive mountain ranges surround it, with peaks of infinite variety and charm, and over all the lofty eminence of Slioch presides with majestic indifference. The Loch itself is studded with fir clad islands, whose rocky shores and sandy beaches provide a pleasing foreground to the distant views of Glen Dochartie, the Torridon range, and Ben Airidh Charr (Ben Arry Char), Tollie Rock and the western mountains. The play of light and shadow, sunshine and storm, over loch and mountain, create a series of pictures which delight the eye, and rise before one in imagination in the dark days of winter. No one can forget its beauty in the noon-day heat of midsummer, when the mountains look almost unreal in the opal light; or again when their rugged outlines are softened and suffused by the mellow light of evening, and the wonderful Alpine glow colours the high tops a deep rose-pink. But there is a sterner side to Loch Maree when the wind rises, and whips its surface to a tumbling mass of " white horses ". On such occasions the wise angler makes for shelter, and may be storm-stayed until the weather moderates or a motor boat comes to the rescue.

Many years ago, a sign was displayed on Loch Maree Hotel, under the Royal Coat of Arms, stating that it was " The finest Loch Fishing in Scotland ". This was removed when the Hotel changed hands in 1925 possibly to spare the

PLATE VII

Loch Maree, Ross-shire

feelings of the unsuccessful angler, or more probably, on the principle that " good wine needs no bush ".

The fishing rights of the first four miles of the Loch belong to Kinlochewe Hotel, but the stretch from Grudie River to Coree on the south side, and to Witches Point on the north side, belongs to Loch Maree Hotel. This expanse is divided into twelve beats, and the angler takes his place on a roster on arrival, and is ensured a fair deal. Previous to the introduction of beats the policy of " the early bird " prevailed, causing an undignified morning scramble to be first away, and imperilling good sportsmanship and happy relations.

Salmon fishing begins in spring, the fish being taken by minnow at Salmon Reach and Grudie River, and in the bay at Kinlochewe. It is not till July that the fly fisher comes into his own, when the run of sea trout up the River Ewe begins, and silvery leaping trout speedily spread over the Loch. Many of the fishing spots are named Kemp Welch's point, the Keeper's Rock, Capt. Hall's Bay, Cox's Bay—scene of an epic struggle with a salmon—Donald's Bay on Kinlochewe water, Hector's Point, Armory Point, Fool's Rock, John Grant's Bank, and so on. The original stories which gave rise to the names have, in many cases, not been recorded, and are lost in the mists of the past. Modern anglers, however, have their own associations with these famous spots, and many a story is told when the boats have returned from the day's sport.

Queen Victoria visited the Hotel in September 1877, thereby adding the glamour of royal patronage to its other attractions.

Her stay is commemorated by a memorial stone opposite the Hotel, suitably inscribed in Gaelic, and in the name of the Victoria Falls, the turbulent stream which pours down the hillside from Loch Gharbhaig to join the Loch at Slatadale. There is also a boulder known as " The Queen's Seat ", a short distance west of the Hotel, which has been preserved as a view-point ever since.

The romantic Isle of Maree is situated in the middle of the Loch, close to its north shore. It is remarkable in many

ways, and differs entirely from the other islands. Closely
wooded with forest trees and hollies planted by the monks, the
crumbling walls of whose monastery still remain, it contains
an ancient burial ground and a wishing tree.

Queen Victoria visited the Island and is reputed to have
placed a gold coin in the wishing tree. It is to be feared,
however, that the royal wish was not fulfilled, as it is a necessary condition that the coin should remain in the tree if the
wish is to be granted.

In the burial ground in the centre of the island are com-
memorative stones to many members of the Maclean family,
and a Celtic Cross to Alexander Robertson of Loch Maree
Hotel and Kinlochewe Hotel, who died in January 1925.
Two flat tombstones with mediaeval crosses mark the graves
of a Norwegian prince and princess, about whom a sad story
is told. The young Prince Olaf was a leader of the Vikings,
and lived an adventurous life on a ship of war. Falling in
love with a beautiful maiden, he feared to ask her to share his
dangerous life, and consulted the holy father at his hermitage
on Isle Maree. The old man counselled the Prince to build
a tower on the Island, to the west of his own cell, which
would serve as a home for them when together, and a safe
retreat for his bride when he put to sea. This was done, and
the marriage was solemnised by the hermit on the Island.
After a time of rapturous happiness, duty called the Prince to
lead forth his men in battle. At parting they arranged that
the Prince should display a white flag on his boat when he
sailed up the Loch to re-join his bride. If he had fallen in
battle a black flag was to be flown. The same signals were
to be given on the Princess's boat as it set out from the island.
During her young husband's absence the Princess became a
prey to doubts and fears, fears as to the loved one's safety, and
doubts of his love. Did a life of adventure hold more attraction for him than the peace and security of their island home?
At length his boat was sighted at Poolewe with the white flag
flying. The Princess set out to meet him but, to test his love,
caused the black flag to be flown and feigned death on an
improvised bier. The trick succeeded too well. As the boats

drew alongside, the Prince jumped aboard and, overcome with grief, stabbed himself with his own dirk. The Princess, stricken by remorse, seized the dirk and also perished by her own hand. If the legend has little significance for us, at least it serves as a warning against the folly of grim practical jokes.

The method of proceeding to the angler's beat for the day has changed with the changing years. Formerly each boat had two ghillies and a pair of long oars, whose steady unhurried sweep seemed to typify the leisurely rhythm of life at the beginning of the century. The motor launch was used to tow the boats to the further beats and frequently was called on to go for boats who would otherwise have been storm-stayed. The out-board engine, however, has changed all that and, previous to the outbreak of war, practically every boat was fitted with one. This greatly simplified the position and made each boat independent, even in a storm. It also helped from the angling point of view, allowing a drift over the beat before the morning breeze had died down, and an interval before going over the ground again. Every sea trout angler knows that to go over the fishing water too often, or under unsuitable conditions, only means disappointment and an empty basket. Among personal recollections one day stands out, a September day of gently falling rain when eleven sea trout and a salmon were taken on Steamer Channel, one of the days when sea trout were on the move and everything seemed to go right.

A notable sea trout was caught by my husband, George R. Donald, on Kinlochewe water on 8th September 1930. It was a female sea trout weighing 12 lbs., and the late G. H. Nall, who read its scales, gave the age as 14½ years. Another big sea trout of 11¼ lbs.—fresh from the sea and covered with sea lice—was caught by him in Grudie Bay one July day; it put up a remarkable fight running out a tremendously long line and jumping repeatedly. I understand that even heavier trout have been caught. He had a rather unusual experience in September 1944 on Loch Maree. On our arrival at the Hotel a lady informed us that she had lost a big trout that afternoon which had taken not only her cast of flies but part of her line, her reel having jammed.   A fortnight later we were fishing on the Isle of Maree Beat when my husband hooked a very lively sea trout.   On getting it on board he found, in addition to his own fly on one side of the mouth, another fly on the other side attached to 9 feet of cast and 15 feet of line, 24 feet in all. The trout had taken the bob fly, leaving the tail fly free.   The trout weighed 4½ lbs., was in perfect condition, and seemingly quite indifferent to this encumbrance.

CHAPTER XIV

WORMING A ROSS-SHIRE BURN

by R. MACDONALD ROBERTSON

There are more things in heaven and earth, Horatio,
Than are dreamt of in your philosophy.
SHAKESPEARE: *Hamlet*

IT WAS the year before the World War started. We were
on our way to the far North on a short fishing holiday and
decided to put up overnight at the very comfortable little
Inn known as The Novar Arms, Evanton, which district,
from boyhood days, has always been well known to me, my
relatives having farmed there for a long number of years.

As the rain had been falling incessantly for several days
previously, we decided to try out the Aultgraat (or Alt Graat
—" ugly burn ") which flows out of Loch Glass at the northern
base of Ben Wyvis, and which, along its whole course seaward,
displays an unbelievable succession of cliffs and waterfalls of
an uncommon character.

The stream, a short distance from the village, on the
estate of Novar, backed by the fine mountain of Fyrish, rushes
down a glacier rut, composed of sandstone strata, for nearly
two miles in length of an average of over one hundred feet in
depth. This remarkable gorge is said to be fully five times
deeper than it is broad. The gully is in many places over-
grown and hidden by thick foliage; while along the rocky
channel below, a roaring torrent is heard rumbling with
violence, though invisible from the banks above. This particular stretch of the stream is locally known as " The Black
Rock of Novar ".

The precipices are green with moss or byssus, which,
like the miner, chooses a subterranean habitat—for here the

75

rays of the sun never fall; the trees, fast anchored in the rock, shoot out their branches across the opening, to form a thick tangled roof at the height of one hundred and fifty feet over-head, while from the recesses within, where the eyes fail to penetrate, there issues a combination of the strangest and wildest sounds ever yet produced by water, there is the deafening rush of the torrent blent as if with the clang of hammers, the roar of vast bellows, and the confused gabble of 1000 voices.

I am informed that many animals have met their doom by falling into this abyss, as the top of it is not fenced off. On one occasion I am told that a dog in pursuit of a roe deer, fell headlong into the chasm; but emerged unscathed several hundred yards further down stream, near the entrance to the Black Rock, wagging its tail. On another occasion it is said that a sailor fell off the bridge—which at one time spanned the head of the ravine—the only man who has ever been known to survive the terrible ordeal. According to the story, he held on to the branch of a tree until rescued by means of a rope, the end of which was lowered to him from the bank up above.

A short distance from the entrance to the Black Rock, there is a cave by the water's edge, only approachable by rope from above. This cavern is situated in the rock at the base of a perpendicular waterfall of some eighty feet in height. The cave in olden days was used for the purpose of making whisky and the fumes from the still were cleverly concealed in the spray of the descending body of water.

On account of the contour of the land at this part of the burn and its steep declivities, it is quite unfishable; therefore, we decided to commence angling operations up-stream some distance above this awesome cauldron.

Picture yourself on a moor with mountains towering all around, some scattered pine trees and heather as far as the eye can reach, with no habitation in sight save a lonely shieling. A burn flowing through the landscape, now pouring through a narrow cleft and forming cascades of the most tempting description, then wandering out on the level in rippling stretches and fascinating pools which leave nothing to be desired. Fly or worm will take—that humble but attractive worm being perhaps the better.

The number of anglers who depend upon the streams of our Scottish Highlands is largely and annually increasing. Many of the burns have not been seriously taxed, as they are for all practical purposes, unknown.

Some anglers talk scornfully of what they term " bait-fishing " and contend that all one has to do is to drop in the " bait " and pull out the trout. One fisher told me that he only fished " bait " once, when he filled every available receptacle with fish, including many strange vessels. Obviously he knew nothing of the higher side of the art, which can be developed only by him who fishes in the burns which flow among our Highland hills. That man was born nineteen centuries and some odd years too late; he should have been with Simon Peter and James and John, the sons of Zebedee, when they got that magnificent haul on the Lake of Gennesaret, in which case he should, I doubt not, have given them several valuable tips! It is impossible to please everybody, and that which is gall to the confirmed fly-fisher, is balm to the habitual angler with the worm; but the worm " dieth not! "

Many Highland rivers, on account of their boulder strewn beds and precipitous banks, render fishing exceedingly difficult for even the most agile and experienced angler. For example, there is the narrow gorge of considerable depth with steep slopes over-grown with thick foliage through which the burn flows in a series of little waterfall-pools, rushes and fascinating swirls. Of such a stream the average angler, keen as he may be, thinks twice before attempting to risk his skin to say nothing of his gear on the hazardous descent. To fish a gully such as this thoroughly, the only way is to get right down to water level and then commence fishing up-stream, as it is useless to attempt angling operations from above. In doing so he will probably be forced to wade, often over his knees, as also to scramble over boulders, scale rocky banks, crawl along ledges of projecting rock overhanging terrifying chasms and struggle through thick undergrowth, all the while balancing his rod until he finally gains access to the next fishable pool.   There are joys and thrills innumerable to the real lover of sport who is willing to risk everything in order to enveigle the wily fish from the inky depths of the mountain stream.   Although the task is often difficult, the sportsman is usually well rewarded for his persistence, for these threatening ravines with awesome cavities frequently yield surprising results of a most unexpected nature.   For sport of this sort, the ideal garb consists of a waterproof fishing jacket (complete with attachment for the landing net) preferably worn with the kilt, and a stout pair of tacketed shoes and thick stockings.   The reputation and advantages of the kilt are two-fold, viz., the spirit it creates in its wearer and the terror the spirit of it gives the enemy knowing its history.

I offer *inter alia* the following seven tips, for what they are worth, to those sportsmen who contemplate a tramp-angling holiday through the Highlands:

1. Rise early in the morning, eat a large breakfast and turn over a good long distance before say, 10 a.m., with a bag full of provisions.

2. Finish the day's work before partaking of a second meal.   Slabs of chocolate and raisins, etc., should be eaten periodically during the day's march.

3. The free use of alcohol should be avoided, as such stimulants produce langour, enervate the frame and do more harm than good.   Water should be partaken in the proper spirit.   Often the incautious angler, without having any craving for liquor, has sacrificed his life to what he considered was the best means of preserving it and of invigorating his exertions. But nevertheless, it is a good precaution to carry a copious flask, although it is unwise to use it in the course of a long day, except perhaps towards the end of the journey or at night before retiring to rest.

4. Do not indulge in drinking too rich milk—a beverage most tempting—often pressed upon the thirsty angler at the instance of kindly Highland crofters.   This is apt to sour the stomach especially during broiling hot weather.

5. Never set out on a day's angling-tramp in new shoes or boots, as these are almost certain to blister the feet.   Foot-

wear should neither be too old nor too new, and the soles should be thick and the leather should have adapted itself, through usage, to the shape of the feet. Before starting out, the footgear should be carefully inspected to see that they afford free ankle movement and that neither nails nor tacket-points are protruding through the soles or the heels. It is often a wise precaution to moisten the inside of the boots or shoes with soft soap and the outside of the leather should be well oiled. The feet should be washed night and morning and thereafter rubbed with " witch hazel " ointment. Socks or stockings should be of a thick woollen texture. The same pair should not be used two days in succession and if they cannot be rinsed and dried each day they should be well aired.

6. A solution of Epsom Salts applied to the exposed parts of the body will ward off attacks by midges and other stinging insects.

7. The kilt is the ideal garb for sport of this kind as it offers to its wearer ample scope for freedom of movement provided no barbed wire fences are likely to be encountered.

If no landing-net is used, a good plan is to hang a basket from your neck in front of you. After you have hooked your fish and allowed him to run for a few seconds, shorten your line to the length of the rod, lift him quietly to the surface and then deftly swing him into the creel. For trout of three or four ounces, this method, once acquired, is unequalled; everything over that weight, however, should be dealt with less summarily, by closing your knees and stooping until they are a few inches under water; then gently guiding the trout into the hollow thus formed, after which the rest is easy more or less. Of course a few trout may be lost through their struggles in mid-air, but this is more than balanced by the time saved. Time is everything, if the angler has promised to return for dinner at a fixed hour. Should he turn up late, however, he is often spoken to with " the tongues of angels "; but it is idle to argue against the voice of women, which is the law of the Medes and Persians! Fault-finding and nagging are terms which imply a habit, unsocial habit or habits, deplorable, depressing and soul-destroying in the eyes of the angler.

After all, there is a difference between fault-finding and finding fault, for the fault-finder is perpetually at it, scattering discouragement and criticism. An angler should never be made small in the eyes of his comrades, and if his wife *must* find fault, it should be with a desire for the real good of her husband. But, alas! too often a reprimand is designed to sting rather than to help; and stinging achieves nothing except to foster hatred in the eyes of the fisher.

The rod used for rough worm fishing should be about ten or eleven feet long, not too supple and capable of throwing a length of line suitable for nearly every variety of pool. The reel should be in proportion to the rod and should render perfect balance. It should have a fairly large drum with light action. The line should neither be too thick nor too bright in colour. Three or four strands of long tapered gut should be neatly tied and whipped on to the end of the tapered line; this will enable the baited hook at the end of the cast to go out much straighter and fall more lightly on the water. Unless the water be drumly, the gut casting-line should not be too thick and not shorter than $2\frac{1}{2}$ feet. The strength of the gut should be determined according to the nature of the stream and the condition of the water. The play of a two-pounder on fine gut is quite equal to that of any 20-lb. " fish " that ever tried to break away with a salmon cast. One or more small split-shot sinkers should be fixed to the casting-line —the first about a foot from the hook, which should be of the single round bend type. The point of the hook should be periodically inspected to see that it has not become blunted.

The deadliest lure for brown trout is the worm commonly known as the " Edinburgh Pink-tail "—a tough little worm of about $2\frac{1}{2}$ inches in length; for sea trout the large black-headed worm and for salmon the large dew-worm. The worms, carried in a cloth bag, should be scoured in dampish moss some days before being used. In baiting, the hook should be covered, leaving the barb to project through the tail part so that the worm can wriggle naturally.

As to conditions of water in which the burn should be fished, no one can lay down a definite set of rules. Good sport is often got where it is least expected. Provided the fisher gets a few scorching cloudless days, with no frost at night, in succession, he will account for many fish if his hand be proficient in the art of up-stream clear-water worm-fishing, though at such times he must use very fine tackle and fish quietly. When the water is low, it is not in every part of a stream where sport may be looked for; but the easiest method is to exhaust the edges of violent rapids by fishing along the sides of the strongest currents, taking advantage of every eddy or other shelter it contains. The angler should gently throw or swing the line up-stream, allowing the bait to drift down with the current, raising the point of the rod slowly as the worm travels down stream, keeping the line moderately taut in order to facilitate striking. On the indication of a nibble, he will be well advised to wait a few moments before striking, to enable the fish to gain a firmer grip of the bait. Once a fish is hooked, it should be gently played towards the angler.

Before wading in, the shallower parts of the stream nearest the angler should be exhausted before the deeper, and the cast increased gradually, best results usually being obtained by fishing runs under banks, near tree roots, and particularly swirls and eddies where the shallow water joins the deep. When a trout is hooked, never attempt to drag it ashore, for if lightly hooked, the moment it reaches the shallow water, it is gone. Many trout will be found in shallow streams, and it is very necessary to keep well out of sight in approaching them. When trout are feeding, they remain only a few inches below the surface and are able to see everything that goes on. As it is only in clear water that much success can be expected, hence up-stream fishing is *de rigueur* and the line should be immersed as little as possible. Amongst good places are those where reefs or large boulders break the flow of some strong current, which afford concealment and shelter to good trout. Large trout always select those spots in a stream where they can get the maximum food with the minimum of trouble.

There is delight unshared by any other class of sportsman, which fills the heart of the fisherman when the first raindrops fall heavily after the shrivelling torture of a long drought. When

G

the burn comes down in spate, the sting of the rain and the leaden sky above do not affect the keen angler in the slightest degree; he walks in earthly paradise. " Great is the reward of the faithful—plump trout for houris and the rushing of the streams for music." He watches the burn redden, and drops his worm daintily into the side of a swirl and feels at once the businesslike tug of the fish and that undefinable quiver of his taut line. Sometimes large trout in broad deep stretches cannot be reached from the bank; but a little flood brings them into the side where the water sleeps in an eddy, or where the fish are waiting to be fed. The line sweeps out and falls in easy circles. There is a momentary glimpse of a white belly and a splashing of water. Then " exit trout " in as dignified a manner as possible! If the river be coloured, there is every chance of a good basket, especially if the water is on the rise, when the fish possess an unusual appetite. During such conditions, when trout are frequently caught sheltering from the current in the quieter sides of the streams, the angler should strictly observe the proverb: " If you dinna see the bottom, dinna wade far oot." Good results are sometimes also obtained by concentrating for a short time on a pool with sandy bays into which the trout come to feed and take refuge from the stronger currents.

Then follows the " Tramp, tramp, squelch, squelch " upstream until nightfall, and after dark the pipe of damp tobacco smoked on the homeward trudge; and afterwards the spreading out of white bellies and red spots on the big plates, the kitchen fire, the casting off of wet clothes, the supper, the dram, and so to bed with head clear but sleepy, and muscles pleasantly tired.

Should permanence be thought a test of truth, the fisher is a true lover. His passion may sleep, but through all his days it never dies. If Hades be peopled with the " shades of men outworn ", the Highland angler's ghost will ever endure to wear the kilt. He will no doubt hire out Charon's ferryboat by the hour and thrash the muddy waters of the Styx for infernal fish. Nor will he be quite happy without his rod even in the Elysian Fields.

That particular day's angling on the flooded water of the Aultgraat river will ever be a living memory for, between us, my friend and myself loaded our baskets with over forty beautifully conditioned red spotted brown trout, some well over ¾ lb. in weight.

Many weird and ghostly stories, local and otherwise, centre round " The Black Rock of Novar " but perhaps the following is amongst the most outstanding:

THE LADY OF BALCONIE

This is the tale of a compact with the Devil.

Many years ago, a young Englishman of noble birth on holiday in Ross-shire, went one night to a Highland Ball at Alness. For some time he sat alone, looking on at the dances which, alas, were foreign to him, when suddenly he noticed a beautiful girl, lovely as a fairy-tale princess, with hair black as night and eyes like dark pools. Soon he found himself asking her to dance; and they took the floor to the lilting strains of a waltz. She was as light as thistledown in his arms, and her slender feet scarcely seemed to touch the floor as she danced. The soft, sweet music and the beauty of his partner acted on the young man like a potent drug. The music ceased, and they wandered arm in arm off the floor. Then he saw a servant approaching to drive the lady home. " Before you go, will you tell me who you are ?" he asked. Smiling sadly, she shook her head and, with a sigh, replied, "Alas, I cannot." Soon the carriage and its fair occupant had disappeared from sight; and, his curiosity piqued, the young man began to question the other dancers about the identity of the lovely lady who looked so sad. " She is the *Lady of Balconie*," he was told. On pressing for further information, he learned that there was a strange mystery about her. She loved to walk alone at night along the banks of the Aultgraat by the Black Rock of Novar, and the fear-haunted surroundings of this dark chasm seemed to possess for her an uncanny fascination. The river after pursuing a winding course through the mountainous parish of Kiltearn runs through a precipitous gulf of great depth. In many places the river is wholly invisible; its voice, however, is ever lifted up in a wild sepulchral wailing, that seems the lament of an imprisoned spirit. The house of Balconie lies within a few miles of this awful chasm.

Disregarding all warnings to shun the spot, he resolved to visit it the next night. His mission was not in vain. He reached the Black Rock as evening was drawing to a close. The surroundings were awesome enough to strike terror into the boldest heart. It was

> A savage place! as holy and enchanted
> As e'er beneath a waning moon was haunted
> By woman wailing for her demon-lover!

Here they met, high above the chasm, and embraced among the swirling wreaths of mist that eddied unceasingly over the edge of the precipice; while round them the night-wind shrieked and moaned like a soul in torment, and far below the waters of the black cauldron seethed in fury.

To the accompaniment of the roaring of the waters, the Lady of Balconie told him her sad story. Some years before, a serious illness, while in her teens, had robbed her of her beauty, of which she was very vain. She had entered into a compact with the Devil that, if he made her the most beautiful of women for the next five years, she would give herself up to him, body and soul, at the end of that time. As soon as the unholy bargain was struck, she had regretted it. She had been lovely and sought after for these five years, but now the time had come for her to fulfil her part of the bargain. It was here that the Devil would come to claim her.

Even as she spoke, a tall white stately figure crowned with horns loomed up before them through the mist, and in commanding tones called the lady to follow him. The young man felt her slipping silently from his grasp over the dizzy brink of the gorge. As she sank from sight she threw a bunch of keys upwards to her lover. Her aim, however, was wide of the mark, and as the keys of Balconie fell back into the depths below, they struck a projecting boulder, on the surface of which they left a permanent indentation. They were red-hot from contact with the Foul Fiend.

With a wild cry of despair, the young Englishman dived after her into the black pool, only to be dashed to pieces on the rocks below.

Long afterwards, an angler belonging to the district, while " worming " his way up-stream in order to lessen the load, took from his basket a number of trout and hid them by the burn side at a spot near the Black Rock. On his return he found that the fish had mysteriously disappeared, all that remained of his catch being a trail of silvery scales along the grass by the river's edge.

Determined to catch the otter, which he imagined responsible for this depredation, he followed the trail, which led downwards over many a slippery ledge to a gloomy cave, the entrance to which was guarded by two large dogs. Inside he could see, busily engaged in baking, a beautiful lady in the dress of a bygone age. Stories he had heard as a boy came back to his mind, and he knew that he was looking on the lovely *Lady of Balconie* who, a century before, had disappeared with such tragic suddenness. When he had recovered from his amazement, he tried to persuade her to flee with him, but with terrified glances behind her, she shook her head and motioned him imperatively away. She thereupon laid hold of a mass of leaven which lay on the table, flung a piece at each of the dogs and waved her hand to the fisherman to leave the cave. After repeated entreaties, the angler sadly bade her farewell, and retraced his steps to the top of the cliff, nor was he ever afterwards able to find the cavern.

Local tradition attributes the disappearance of the Lady of Balconie

to none other than *Domhnull Dubh*, the Prince of Darkness himself, and he
it is, they say, who keeps her prisoner.   When the mists swirl among the
tree-tops over the ravine, the villagers say that she is busy at her baking,
and on moonlight nights when the river is in flood and the wind moans in
the gullies, her wistful shade is to be seen at the Black Rock, searching for
her English lover.

> They named it Aultgraat—Ugly Burn,
> This water through the crevice hurled
> Scouring the entrails of the world—
> Not ugly in the rising smoke
> That clothes it with a rainbowed cloak.
> But slip a foot on frost-spiked stone
> Above this rock-lipped Phlegethon
> And you shall have
> The Black Rock of Kiltearn
> For tombstone, grave,
> And trumpet of your resurrection.

CORRIE HALLOCH

Measach Falls, Near Ullapool, West Ross-shire

The hell of waters, where they howl and hiss,
　　And boil in endless torture—while the sweat
Of their great agony, wrung out from this,
　　Their Phlegethon, curls round the rocks of jet,
　　That grid the gulph around in pitiless horror set.

Byron's *Childe Harold*, canto 4, stanza 69

A somewhat serious tragedy occurred at Corrie Halloch some years ago, when timber cutting was in progress at the Braemore Estate.

A horse hauling a large larch log along the path on the north side of the chasm, met an untimely end when the whole bank (which was badly undermined at this part) suddenly collapsed. The hapless animal fell to its doom some three hundred feet into the gloomy depth of the " Filthy Hollow ", and was lost in the Stygian abyss below. The carcase of the horse was eventually washed seawards by heavy floods.

Owing to the contour of the *locus*, it was quite impossible either to attempt a rescue or to recover the creature. The man who was leading the horse had a very narrow escape.

So far as is known, and I have sounded a number of local people on the subject, no one other than the writer of the article which follows, has ever been known to attempt to fish the gorge immediately below the major fall, which takes an almost perpendicular leap of approximately 275 feet.

CHAPTER XV

PETER AND I IN THE CORRIE HALLOCH

by V. CARRON WELLINGTON

L ooking down into the inky depths of the pool below the Falls of Measach, I felt that irresistible desire to go down and fish it, and reviewed the precipitous and forbidding rock walls with trepidation, and decided that a descent near the bridge spanning the falls was impossible. The prospect of descending about half a mile down-stream looked better, although this entailed as wild and dangerous a scramble back up-stream that no sane-minded angler would wish for. It was the only way to arrive at the Falls Pool.

Having decided on this course, I advised my friends of my intention, and told them to expect me back at the hotel about sunset. A precautionary measure which sounded like making my last will and testament in the event of . . .

The day was warm and sunny, and my garb of a pair of light khaki shorts and a thin open-necked shirt suited the adventure admirably, and comparable with a two-piece swim-suit. Having exercised my prerogative as a Highlander, I cut myself a strong thumb-stick to which I lashed my wee Hardy eight-footer and collapsible landing net, and proceeded in search of a reasonable looking spot to descend into the gorge. It commenced tough, and tougher still was my arduous progress up that turbulent water, which smashed itself against the boulders and precipitous cliffs which sometimes afforded only narrow, sloping, slithery ledges at varying heights above this spate-furied rush of water. The alternative was a cold plunge, a short swim, or a 50 to 100 foot climb and descent, both of which were frequently indulged in during the one and a half hours gruesome and strenuous passage. It was darned cold in that gorge, the going was dangerous

87

work, demanding every care and precaution and no foolish pranks, not that I could think of anything more foolish than the adventure itself.

I reached my objective, if not quite exhausted, feeling pretty tired. As I rested a wee while at the tail of the pool, my upward glance was met by a very narrow streak of cloudy sky, and two people standing on the suspension bridge looked dwarfed to marionettes by the height. The gorge looked so much narrower from below, and I felt I had descended into some hellish pit, engulfed by these overpowering cliffs that seemed to terminate in the sky like a pair of railroad lines that merge into one straight stretch of a permanent way. The roar of the falls in full spate was terrifying, and the whole place vibrated with the terrific force of millions of gallons of furious foam hurling itself from the rocky shelf three hundred feet above. If this pool looked weird and forbidding from the bridge above, it certainly looked a thousand times more so from where I stood.

I was cold, wet through, and thoroughly miserable, cursing myself quietly for having undertaken such a mad adventure. It had nothing to do with bravado; but that urge to cast a fly in impossible places, and curiosity about the result. I was frightened, too, we all are sometimes, but I'm admitting it, and there were brief moments when I couldn't see myself ever getting out of the place again, either dead or alive. The continuous roar of the falls was nerve-racking, deafening. I yelled out at the top of my voice but never heard a thing.

Having blazed my trail so far, I decided to make my rod. I thought my trembling fingers would never succeed in tying my cast and fly. A 2 × level and a medium " Peter Ross ".

The most convenient cast I could hope for was a slithery, narrow ledge standing about three feet above water a little higher than mid-pool and to which I had to crawl barefooted on my hands and knees, thinking all the while that if once I slipped into that swirling inkpot of unknown depth, I might easily be dragged below in the clutches of some monstrous devils bequeathed by some vile witches so long associated

PLATE VIII

The Great Measach Fall—" Corrie Halloch," Ullapool, W. Ross-shire

with the gorge. Very cautiously I rose on my feet, and stood
there perched and bobbing like a water-ousel, feeling far less
secure and wishing I had its wings to carry me out of the place.
I was truly scared and unnerved, and decided to return without
a single cast. But cast I did eventually, and my courage was
revived a little as I felt the unseen contact with my first
attempt, just a wee touch of a fish as curious as myself, both
seeking the same trouble. It came again to my third with
definite interest, but I was nervy and slow and far too late in
striking. Whether it was the same fish or not I cannot tell,
but five minutes later I was enjoying the prelude to a " Sonata
in Screams Major on my Hardy's Perfect " as my line virtually
cut the pool water like a knife through butter. Back it came
from the head like lightning and away to the far side of the
tail, then back again to the head as he probably realised that
there was a strange and restraining power at the other end of
the line. Here it sulked for about ten minutes (or was it
ten years ?) before it moved and repeated the runs twice over
before condescending to come alongside to ascertain what
was really worrying him at the other end. Poor devil, he was
as much in a panic as I had been, and was about to be. It was
fully fifteen minutes before I got a glimpse of his jet black
dorsal and the realisation that there was still some fight in
him. It was hopeless to try and net him from my perilous
position three feet above, so decided to worry him a little
longer, and finally got him along, tummies up, dropped my
rod on the ledge, and with my left hand gripping a small
projection of rock, and a prayer that it would hold, I got
down on my tummy and reached over the ledge and swung
him up beside me. He squirmed, but the net held him, the
whole $3\frac{1}{2}$ lbs. of his black ugly body. On my hands and
knees I crawled back to the tail of the pool, pushing rod and
fish in net before me. I couldn't drive away the thought that
something or other would get hold of my right foot which
was dragging over the ledge, and pull me in. I found myself
continually looking back to make sure. Sounds foolish maybe,
but as the reader, you were not in my foolish predicament
and I don't advise you to follow my example. Having

administered the last rites I left him on the ledge and decided that I couldn't possibly return to the same position.

My second attempt was less precipitous to land a fish, and this I made from a pine log that had fallen some time ago across the tail of the pool. In a cast or two " Peter " was once again in contact with a " Foolish One " and the combat was very much akin to the former, concluding in about ten minutes with another black devil of $2\frac{3}{4}$ lbs.

With my courage renewed, and even my somewhat precarious world forgotten, I was settling down to enjoy myself. I forgot I was wet and cold, that my teeth chattered, and my brain vibrated with the constant roar of the falls that seemed angrier than ever. I was about to try for my third nigger, when I became obsessed with the idea that the falls were getting angrier and were doing their utmost to reach me, at this moment a black, heavy cloud must have passed over the gorge completely obscuring the sun, or I should say, the light, since the sun never sets on the waters in this gorge. It cast as weird and deathly a gloom over the gorge as no man or beast was ever intended to see. I felt I had intruded on something terrible, and was about to pay the penalty for it. I confess I panicked, dropped my rod and turned tail, but I had not got very far when something urged me to return and collect my tackle. I debated the advisability of taking the fish lest the terrible hands of vengeance should follow me, but take them I did. I broke my rod and lashed it, and gill-strung the fish to my waist-belt, and commenced my journey down-stream with a feeling of fright such as no battlefield or London blitz had caused. I remember the special caution I took with every step, feeling that if I once slipped and fell in, " they " would be waiting for me. I was half way back before I rested. The gorge had widened a bit and the cloud had passed over, things looked brighter and more hopeful. As I rested beside the pool there was a rise, such a one that an angler dreams about. I could not resist it, made my rod again and sent " Peter " for another ride from the head of the pool. He sank deeper than usual before reminding me that he was in contact with another lively combatant, whose fighting tactics were commensurate with the former catches and with a similar power of endurance. He was a cleaner fish and turned the scale at 1½ lbs.

" Peter " was getting a bit battle-scarred, but he was game for another cast and proved his attractive merits within five minutes, but lost his laurels five minutes later when for some unseen reason he let go. Back we went into the battle, and for quite ten minutes he lost sight of the enemy. I was about to relieve him of his command, when suddenly as he dangled on the edge of the pool while I sought another fly, a playful young trout invited him to come out and play again. He was certainly " taken " for a ride this time, and it was only by sheer luck that my rod didn't follow him. " Peter " knew he was in disgrace and was determined to retrieve his error— might have been mine, of course—and finally presented me with a very nice 1½ lb. beauty as a peace offering.

Time was getting on, I was tired, chilly, and thought it advisable to move on and seek the sun and warmth. I proceeded down-stream to the point where I had earlier descended, and near a very likeable pool. Thought I'd try one more cast before leaving and sent " Peter " on patrol once more. He proved as good a scout as ever, and judging by what was going on in those unseen depths, I concluded that he was in combat with something more than he had bargained for. This chap tugged away like a mad terrier into a rat, but " Peter " held on like grim death as my frail little eight-footer nodded like a willow in a stormwind. We were a good team, and backed " Peter " up for all we knew as this unseen adversary began to race up and down the pool. He tired, rested and sulked a little, then up he came again and took " Peter " for another ride, concluding with as fine a display of aquatic acrobatics as I've ever seen. It was fully ten minutes since he commenced the offensive and went down for another sulk, then slowly, but firmly he made his way to the tail of the pool which terminated in a strongish cataract. This was my sixth fish averaging a ten minute strenuous combat on my frail 2 × cast, and I knew that if he got over those falls that I could bid him a " cheeriebye ".

Over he did go and into the pool below. My 30 yard
Kingfisher was all out and accompanied with about 20 yards
of backing. I held on hopefully as hard as I dared, trusting
in exhaustion and lack of stamina to revive. It was impossible
to follow him from where I stood. My rod was almost a
hoop when I decided to hand-line him and trust to the gods.
He broke me at the cast and away went my adversary to spend
the rest of his days with my dear old " Peter ". He was as
game a trout as I've ever been in contact with and I don't
begrudge him his well earned victory, but I do bemoan the
loss of my faithful old friend " Peter " whom I should have
liked to keep as a souvenir of what in my humble opinion was
one of the most exciting, exhausting, soul-scaring and mad
adventures one could wish to experience in the torrential
waters of the Western Highlands. I am not in the least
ashamed to confess that I was scared out of my skin, and that
a King's stretch on the Dee for the rest of my life would never
induce me to repeat it—at least, that is how I feel about it
just now—in any case never alone.

Half an hour later found me beside my cycle near the little
green gate, looking the worse for wear and wondering if my
four fish were really worth it. I think so!

THE BONNIE BRAES OF ULLAPOOL

I long to look at the hills again
  And the lochs in their sunlight fun;
I long to hear the curlew's call
  And the burns on their tinkling run:
My ears are strained for the cataract's roar
  And my eyes for their peat-stained foam:
I long for the breeze that cooled my brow,
  Och! How my heart longs to roam.

I long for the tuneful chant of the birds
  And the ease they gave to my load;
My heart content, with cromak and rod,
  Full of song on the open road.
I miss the scent of the bracken, too,
  And the whir of startled wings;
Leaves in the breeze beneath the sun,
  Wonderful, Godly things.

I long to be back in this hilly land
  For the climb, and the rocky slope
That leads me where I cannot see,
  But only trust and hope.
On unknown tracks to summits
  Where kingdoms I survey;
The glory of God's own garden,
  And the Isles across the bay.

I long to reach the border line
  Abreast with the lark in flight;
Where gulls hand over to the hawk
  And shun the eagle's might.
Higher and higher, o'er corrie and crag,
  Aye! Higher still would I be
To feel the breeze, and God's good sun
  Or the small rain from the sea.

I long to see the deep blue lochs
  High up on the peat-bogged hills,
To make my rod, and with chosen fly
  Prepare for the bite that thrills:

Happy, contented, I cast the day long
    With carefree songs in my heart;
Good fish in the creel, the sun deep west,
    For my long trek home, I depart.

Oh, for the bark of a shepherd's dog
    Or the bleat of a lonely sheep;
The wondering gaze of a shaggy herd
    And a covey tailing for sleep.
The scent of the myrtle, squelch of peat,
    The purple of bonnie heather,
Och! I long to blaze these trails again.
    Just God and me—together.

True, I may wander the hills alone,
    But I'm never " alone " on the hills.
Their charm and enchantment grip my soul
    And they're peopled from God's own mills.
In wonder and awe, I bare my head
    And ask, for my soul's relief—
" Why, Lord, makest all so fair to behold
    And the span of my life so brief? "

I miss the danders at eventide
    To the bridge above the mill,
The lullaby of the corrie burn,
    When all was hushed and still.
The deep red sun that fired the West
    Beyond the Summer Isles.
As much as these, I know I miss
    Some folk, and their friendly smiles.

I feel like a bird, crying for space,
    Or the deer in a keeper's pen,
Gasping for breath like a netted trout,
    Restless, in my city den.
Though toss I must in the ebb and flow
    Of the sea of maddening strife,
I shall always long for the hills again,
    Their peace, contentment and life.

V. Carron Wellington

CHAPTER XVI

WEST SUTHERLAND FISHING HAUNTS

by R. MACDONALD ROBERTSON

SUTHERLAND, the haunt of Kings and a retreat of Premiers, has a strange and fascinating effect on the mind of the average tourist. It has a distinct appeal and creates a longing to return.

Tucked away in the far north-west corner of Scotland where the railway does not yet penetrate, lies a land unspoilt by the hand of man, of particular charm on account of its dark, broody glens, its individual peaks, its rushing rivers and savage cascades, and principally on account of its inaccessibility and the adventure of getting there.

A journey due west from Invershin to Lochinver and thence due north to Durness following the coast road (or as an alternative route from Lairg—" The Pass ", by Lochs Shin, Merkland, More and Stack to Laxford—" Fiord of Salmon ") and from there on to Tongue and Bettyhill should convince the traveller that in Sutherland alone can be found a variety of scenery which can safely be said to " overawe and uplift the soul ".

Loch Shin possesses a peaceful charm in contrast to the wilder aspect of Lochinver—" Loch-an-inbhir " (The Loch of the River mouth) with the massive bulk of Suilven (Norse " Piller-fell " or " Eye-like Ben ") the Sentinel towering high above it, while Elphin—the " Heights of Assynt " can surely be classed as a Trout Angler's Paradise. Inchnadamph is famous for three things: (1) Caves in which have been discovered prehistoric remains; (2) an underground river and (3) the source of a river which gushes out of the side of a hill— the purest crystal-clear water in Scotland. Travelling due north from Lochinver along the coast road via Stoer and

Kylesku, one passes the beautiful bays of Achmelvich, Clachtoll, Clashnessie, Nedd and Ardvar. At the head of Loch Glencoul in a solitary den of nature is a waterfall believed to be more than three times the height of Niagara called Eas-Coul-Aulin which, when in flood, can rival many of the famous cataracts of the world. North of Kylestrome one encounters a " Highland chaos "—Eddrachillis being perhaps the wildest and most rugged Parish in Scotland, and on the road north of Scourie conical peaks become ridges, while ridges in turn mount into cones, for the mountains are all separated from each other and loom up darkly from a sea of lochans. Scourie (Norse Sker-je " Skerray ") is a seaport village, and stands on a small bay of its own name and opens upon the romantic Island of Handa, which possesses some of the finest rock formations in the county, where myriads of sea-birds whiten its gigantic cliffs. Some years ago, when the Island was inhabited, the oldest woman on it was termed " Queen of the Handa ".

" In the sixteenth century a branch of the Mackays took possession of the south-western part of what came to be called Lord Reay's country, and adopting Scourie as the seat and centre of their influence, assumed the designation of the Mackays of Scourie. One of the race was Lieutenant-General Hugh Mackay, the celebrated commander-in-chief in the reign of William and Mary. He was to have been ennobled by the title of Earl of Scourie, but lost favour at Court through the intrigues of his rival, Mackenzie of Cromarty."

Tropical palms flourish all the year round at Scourie, reckoned to be the farthest north palms in the world and the purest air is said to be found there, where one is able to enjoy the balmy Atlantic breezes.

The Parish of Kinlochbervie (Cean-loch " head of loch ", Norse Bergje " rocky "), situated on the north side of Loch Inchard, is perhaps the most picturesque in Scotland, containing over 150 splendid fishing lochs. Loch Sandwood, some eight miles south of Cape Wrath (with the ruined homestead of the Mackays of Sandwood) and Sandwood Bay are unrivalled in all Scotland on account of their weird and

fascinating surroundings, while Durness (Norse Dyranes
" wild animal headland ") a short distance farther north,
affords a charming sea-side holiday centre. (Before 1742
the Parish of Durness was known as Lord Reay's Country—
Duthaich-Mhic-Aoi—The Land of the Mackays). Nearby is
the famous Cave of Smoo (" Smutha," meaning the Largest
Cave) " Smowe," referred to by Sir Walter Scott in his diary,
dated 19th August, 1814. This Cave is divided into several
inter-communicating compartments which stretch underground for about half a mile. Through a hole in the roof of
the second chamber the Smoo Burn descends perpendicularly
in a waterfall of approximately one hundred feet in semi-
darkness, and many traditions linger round it. The Freisgall
Caves, Loch Eriboll are also well worthy of particular mention,
a number of which also penetrate underground a similar
distance. The mouth of one is obscured by a waterfall.

The west portion of the North Coast of Scotland is indented
by a number of sea-inlets (or fiords), e.g., the Kyle of Durness
(Sango Bay and Rispond), Loch Eriboll and the Kyle of
Tongue (Tung—" Narrow neck "). Two mountain ranges
rise abruptly from the sea on either side of the Great Valley
of Tongue and stretch along its whole length until finally
baulked by Ben Loyal (Queen of Scottish Mountains) and its
terraces of Craig Meircan and Cray-na-Garbat, while gigantic
Ben Hope (3061 feet) looms up in the southern extremity in
romantic grandeur. A little farther east is the peaceful little
hamlet of Bettyhill (named after Elizabeth, Countess of
Sutherland) with its silver sands, sublimely situated, at the
head of Farr Bay. The scenery here is unsurpassable in
beauty and on a clear starry night it may be said that:

> Soft stillness and the night
> Become the touches of sweet harmony.

H

WITH ROD IN SUTHERLAND

by PHILIP GUNN

THERE is no place in Scotland that surpasses Lairg for anglers. Lairg is also a convenient centre for tourists. The situation of the Hotel is particularly beautiful as it stands on a small hill at the south-east end of Loch Shin which stretches away to the north-west for about twenty miles. It is possible to fish all the lochs in the neighbourhood within a radius of fifteen miles with considerable ease. To lovers of the gentle art, Lairg is certainly worth a visit. The river Shin joins the Oykell close to Invershin, and is one of the finest angling rivers in the County. Its trout are not of any consequence, but its quality of salmon cannot be beaten in any part of Scotland and they give capital sport. The angling in the river Oykell is also first class. As many as sixteen salmon have been killed in a day by one rod. This river contains abundance of grilse and trout. The scenery in the vicinity of Inveran and Invershin is magnificent and the Sutherland side of the Kyle presents a pleasant alternation of wood and cultivated fields. The trout in Loch Shin, which generally weigh three to the pound, sometimes reach as high an average as 3 lbs., and *salmo-ferox* are numerous and range from four to fifteen pounds. Lochs Craggie and Doula are excellent trouting lochs. It is quite common for one rod to capture thirty pounds weight of trout averaging from two to three pounds, in a day, and all of surpassing symmetry and beauty. These trout seem to be of a different variety from those obtained in any other loch in Sutherland. They are deep set fish, thickly covered with large brown and orange spots. Lochs Beannach, Tigh-na-creige, Cracail and Dulidh n' Airb also afford good sport. In addition to the lochs mentioned, there are several other smaller lochs in the vicinity, nearly all of which contain trout which give excellent sport. The upper reaches of Loch Shin, as well as Lochs Griama, Merkland and Fiag, are usually fished from Overscaig. These lochs have splendid red-fleshed trout which are sometimes caught as high as 3 lbs. in weight on the fly. *Salmo-ferox* of 12 lbs. have often been taken on the troll. The trout in Loch Fiag weigh up to as much as 4 lbs. The scenery surrounding these lochs is very fine, Ben Hee standing out prominently among the peaks around it. Angling on Lochs Assynt, and on the Sciag, Traligill and Loanan waters is very good. In Loch Assynt the trout average 1 lb., the *salmo-ferox* up to 14 lbs., and salmon are frequently taken. The River Inver flows out of Loch Assynt, and there are splendid beats on this water where salmon can be caught. On the Kirkaig, on which there are about two dozen good angling pools, as many as ten salmon have been taken in a day by one rod alone; but the river is a late one, July to September being the best months. Besides Loch Assynt, Lochs Culag, Beannach, Crocach, Fionn, Veyatie and many others in the neighbourhood yield trout in abundance, especially lochs Crocach and Fionn which contain large trout running from six to ten pounds. Borralan (Altnacealdach) contains good sized trout, also Lochs Fada, Cama and Urigill as well as the rivers Ledbeg and Ledmore. At the base of Ben More lies Loch Gillaroo—the home of the famous trout so eagerly sought by fishers. There is a common belief among anglers that on these seldom fished waters the trout impatiently await the angler's flies. It is not so and on many of these lochs the trout are wild and dour. One may fish for hours on a surface unbroken by a rise. A rise on many of these lochs does not last long. In the circumstances it is a wise policy and one which invariably gives good results to keep changing one's cast of flies periodically which should always include a Peter Ross or Butcher fly to one of Nymphs.

CHAPTER XVII

ANGLING IN REMOTER SUTHERLAND

by R. MACDONALD ROBERTSON

THE HEIGHTS OF ASSYNT (that Brown Trout Angler's Paradise comprising Lochs Borralan, Awe, Urigill, Cama, Veyatie and Assynt) are paramount in perfection from the angler's point of view. Without exaggeration, in one single day in 1937, Sydney Latimer, Edinburgh, landed three *Salmo-ferox* on Loch Assynt weighing respectively 10 lbs., 11½ lbs. and 12¾ lbs. on a 2½-inch unweighted "Tiger" Phantom Minnow, as well as a heavy basket of smaller brown trout on the fly.

So far as Loch Veyatie is concerned, in July 1938, while fishing from the Altnacealdach Hotel, my friend the Rev. Walter E. Lee, D.D., formerly minister of St. John's, Perth, took with rod and line, a *ferox* of 16 lbs. This brown trout was in capital condition and did not have the appearance of an old fish. It was 2 ft. 9 ins. in length and at three different parts was 17-18 ins. in girth. His ghillie was Murdo Macdonald of Elphin.

Loch Veyatie is said locally to be haunted by a Water Monster which dwells in the part immediately below the Black Falls. As very large trout have been captured in this loch, it is quite feasible that the alleged Monster of Loch Veyatie is just a monster brown trout. According to Dr. Lee:

It had been wet weather during my stay at Altnacealdach, and when I reached Loch Veyatie, I found that there was a fairly stiff westerly breeze blowing in my face up the water, so I decided to row in the teeth of the wind and get some drifts back to the anchorage. My boatman suggested that as it would be a stiff pull, I should have a try with the minnow, therefore I went over to the burn which feeds the loch and caught a couple of small trout, one of which I affixed to an "Archer Spinner" which I trolled behind the boat. We had not rowed many hundreds of yards when there

PLATE IX

Photo by courtesy of the E.P.N.

Cast of Brown Trout—weight, 16 lbs.; length, 32 ins.; girth, 23 ins.

This fish was caught on Loch Veyatie, Sutherland, in July 1938, by Rev. Walter E. Lee, D.D., Edinburgh

was a strong pull and the splutter of a big trout; but I never dreamt of so large a fish as it turned out to be.   It was well hooked in the roof of the mouth and I had a stout line.   The difficulty was not so much to get it near the boat, but to land it.   My small net was useless and I did not think of running the boat aground in order to grass the monster, as I should have done; but decided to haul the fish aboard by the gills and we managed this at the second attempt.   It is easy to imagine my surprise and delight when he turned the scales at 16 lbs.   I believe there is no record of a larger trout being caught on Veyatie than this one.   He measured nearly a yard in length and was about half as much in girth.   A cast of this fish was made by an Inverness firm and it now adorns the lounge of the Hotel at Altnacealdach.

Let me now pass on to two other splendid fishing districts in the west of Sutherland which lie more or less off the beaten track.   They are (1) the Stoer and (2) the Kinlochbervie territories, both of which, owing to their remoteness, are fortunately unspoilt, and on this account merit special reference.

In the *quoad sacra* Parish of Stoer in Assynt (which is situated some six and a half miles north-west of Lochinver) there is a perfect network of fresh water lochs.   The majority of these lochans contain brown trout with an occasional salmon.   Permission to fish some of these may be obtained by guests who stay at hotels in the neighbourhood; but from my experience by residing at Croft boarding houses in the same district (which have acquired fishing-rights on a few of the *lesser known* lochans), given a favourable opportunity, brown trout of exceedingly high average weight may sometimes be caught.   In the Stoer district alone, for example, there are four little known, yet outstanding lochs:

Loch na Claise contains brown trout which rise to the fly up to and over 3 lbs. weight.   The big ones which lie near the rushes in the west end require careful stalking and playing.   On occasions salmon enter this tarn up the burn (when in flood) which flows out of this loch into the sea; but the burn has its obstructions, being in several places badly silted up.   Were this stream regularly cleaned out, salmon would obtain better and more frequent access to this lochan.

Loch Froaich, about one and a half miles long by a half mile broad, contains grand red-spotted trout up to and over 4 lbs., which are grand fighters.

Loch Leatha Bhaile Fhoghair (or Laxie). A mysterious little lochan which yields plump red-spotted trout up to and over 3 lbs.; but they are dour to rise.

Loch na Huidhe Doimhne is an inaccessible little lochan with steep shelving banks and deep holes and lies hidden in a den of nature amid wild scenery. Although the average size of brown trout is ½ lb. much larger trout rise to the fly.

All these lochs fish well during a drizzle of rain with a westerly breeze, and Palmer spiders and Worm flies are recommended. The best months are from June to September. These lochans contain brown trout which are exceptionally strong fighters, usually leaping several times into the air before they can be brought to net. These lochs may be dour at times; but an occasional trout of 3 lbs. or over, is worth a dozen half-pounders! In early June 1937 I had, on the fly—despite the cold weather and lack of sufficient breeze— more than one trout of 3 lbs. from these lochs; but brown trout of very much heavier weight are often captured in this district especially on the troll. This is, of course, where trolling is permitted. The most successful cast of flies for the Stoer lochs is one consisting of three different Palmer-spiders or Pennells and, as an alternative, a cast of 2 × gut containing an Alexandra Glory (in tandem) on the bob, the Peter Ross on the mid, and the Worm-fly with the red-tip on the tail. Splendid deep-sea fishing can be enjoyed about a mile out, on a sand-bank right opposite the ancient Broch of Clachtoll, but the tides are very strong.

Kinlochbervie is a Parish of roughly 270 square miles, probably the most picturesque in Scotland, and dotted throughout with over 150 splendid fishing lochs. Looking east south-east from the prominence of Beallach-Tigh-Foinghal, can be observed a panorama of mountains, so wonderful that they literally uplift the soul. Among them are Foinne Bheinn, Meall a Chuirn, Arkill and Stack; while the peaks of Assynt, Glasbheinn, Cuinneag, Canisp and Suilven form a sinister amphi-theatre in the grim background. This hamlet lies on the lower part of the north side of Loch Inchard, three and three quarter miles north-west of Rhiconich and some forty-five

PLATE X

Sandwood Bay, near Kinlochbervie, Sutherland

miles north-west of Lairg. The lochans in this Parish are now locally termed " The Garbet Waters ", formerly attached to the shooting lodge, now a syndicate hotel. In this district are a number of excellent salmon and sea trout lochs, the following of which are worthy of particular mention:

Loch *Sandwood*, derived from the Norse " Sand-vatn " or Sand-water;

Lochs Garbet Mor and *Garbet Beg*;

The General's Loch; and

Loch Aisir Mor and *Innis-na-Ba-Buidhe*.

Loch Sandwood, in my opinion, is paramount on account of its inaccessability, being some fifty miles from the nearest railway station. It is superbly situated amid wild and desolate scenery and is roughly one mile long by approximately half a mile in breadth. It contains good brown trout and an occasional salmon. But here again the burn which connects this loch with the sea is badly silted in places with sand. This loch is fed by the River Shinnery. On leaving the loch, after wending its way " along the trend of the shore ", the stream finally empties itself into the clear blue waters of Sandwood Bay—the most north-westerly beach on the mainland of Great Britain, roughly six miles as the crow flies, south of Cape Wrath. (Cape Wrath derives its name from the Norse word Hvarf meaning a " turning point ".) On the south bank of Loch Sandwood can be seen the ruined homestead of the last of the Mackays of Sandwood. I have visited this bay in stormy weather when the Atlantic combers lashed their creamy furies on the beach and I have walked along its shore bathed in the tranquillity of summer sunshine, and on each occasion I have been more and more impressed by the weird desolation of the windswept scene. Sandwood Bay has the reputation of being haunted, and I am informed that even to-day some of the local inhabitants will not venture near it after sun-down. May I recommend those who seek seclusion and romance to visit Sandwood. The peat road to Loch a' Mhuilinn (the Mill Loch—which recalls the long forgotten past when the local people thirled their corn there) is not too bad to travel over on wheel, after which about a mile's easy walk due northward, through the heather, past Loch Meadhonach and Loch Clais-nan-Coinneal and finally the bent grass of the sandhills, brings one to the desolate but peaceful scene which I have described.

Nearer Richonich there are (1) *Loch Garbet Mor*, about two miles long by a quarter of a mile broad, beautifully situated and draining into Loch Garbet Beg, out of which the River Inchard flows. This loch contains salmon and trout and fishes best in July and August; and (2) *Loch Garbet Beg* lies amid charming scenery. It is about a mile and a half in length and not very wide, and contains salmon grilse and sea trout. At the south-east end, the Narrows fish best from the bank in a stiff breeze. July and August are the best months. According to records, some years ago, one man killed in a day two salmon, thirty-eight sea trout, two grilse and several fine brown trout.

There are also many other nameless mountain tarns in the district near Achlyness and on the north-west side of Foinne Bheinn, all of which yield brown trout *above average size*; but the following (on the road to Sandwood) are outstandingly good:

Loch Larach, which yields heavy fish.

Loch Chraisg, which contains large silvery beauties.

Loch na Gainimh (now known as " Lorna "); and

Loch nan Sac, a grand back o' beyond trouting loch.

Also a series of splendid hill lochans west of Foinaven and several others in Ceathramh Garbh (" The Rough Quarter ") north-west of Achlyness.

To the unexperienced fisher, a word of warning: Should, perchance, he hook a big one, go easy with him, and in playing him, give the fish plenty butt and lots of time. Let the fish run to his heart's content and exhaust him thoroughly before attempting to draw him to the gaff or landing-net.

All the Kinlochbervie lochs fish best after a spate with a north-west breeze. From experience, the same flies which I have recommended for the Stoer lochs, will act equally well on the Garbet waters for ordinary brown trout. For salmon and sea trout the following flies are particularly deadly: (Small size) Jock Scott, Green Highlander and Silver Wilkinson.

WEIRD TALES
OF THE KINLOCHBERVIE DISTRICT

The story is told by legends old,
And by withered dame and sire,
When they sit secure from the winter's cold
All round the evening fire.

The mer-folk were the traditional inhabitants of the briny deep. There are few accounts of mermen; but Highland and Island lore teems with allusions to the mermaids who dwelt

Fathoms deep beneath the wave,
Stringing beads of glistening pearl.

and who often came up from the sea-caves to disport themselves on the shore, and were to be seen in the quiet bays, floating on the surface of the water near Kinlochbervie and mingling their voices with the sighing breeze.

SANDY GUNN AND THE MERMAID

This story was told to me in Gaelic by the late Alexander Gunn, Balchreick, Kinlochbervie, who, in June 1939, was introduced to me by my friend Donald MacLeod, the former Laird of the district.

The mermaid in question is alleged to have been seen by Mr. Gunn off *Ruadh an Fhir Leithe*, and his statement to this effect is corroborated by witnesses who were present at the interview during which I took down notes for the following story, which has nothing whatever to do with any other account of the alleged happening which may have been previously published.

The district of *Sandwood*, in north-west Sutherland, described by Seton Gordon as " the most beautiful place on all the west coast of Scotland," has been called " The Land of the Mermaids "; and it is without doubt a perfect setting for such supernatural beings. Hundreds of waves rush constantly shorewards, falling exhausted upon a beach of great sand-dunes that stretches for miles in both directions. There is nothing for the eye but mingling shades of grey; and nothing for the ear but the rush and roar of the waves.   Sign of life is nowhere visible.   Travellers have told of " singing sands "; those of Sandwood do not sing, but whisper with every rustle of the breeze as they slide over the shattered hulks of ships which lie half-buried all along the beach.   Over all is a sense of unbelievable solitude and desolation.   Only the gulls scream overhead, like the souls of drowned mariners lured to their death by the maidens of the sea.

According to Alexander Gunn:

On the 5th of January (Old Christmas night) 1900, I was going round after sheep between Sheigra and Sandwood Loch.

While walking along the edge of the rocky head-lands, I noticed that one of my sheep had fallen down a gully about three miles south-west of Sandwood Bay, known as *Ruadh an Fhir Leithe;* and as it was low tide, I descended the cliff towards the seashore to take it up.

When I reached the bottom my collie dog suddenly let out an agonised howl as it crouched in terror close into my feet for protection, with hair bristling, ears set back, and tail between its legs.

I looked up.   What I saw was so sudden and unexpected that it took my breath away, for to my astonishment, I observed right above me what I at first took to be a human being reclining on a ledge of rock only about six or seven feet from where I stood.   Then I realised that it was a mermaid!

So impressed was I that I can to this day distinctly recall her appearance which left a vivid picture on my mind which I can never forget, old man as I am.   She was no grey seal; she was a real mermaid—a bonnie lassie, clear in complexion as ever I saw.   Her hair was reddish-yellow in colour, and curly; and she had a wreath of seaweed round her neck.   She had greenish-blue eyes, and arched eyebrows, and she stared at me with a kind of frightened expression on her face.   I remember her appearance distinctly she had a dark yellowish body the colour of the yellow tangle on the seashore.

Like myself, she also got a fright.   She never moved, not even her wee short arms, as she reclined amid the noise of the surf with her fish-like tail dangling over the other side of the rock.   She did not speak.

I sensed the situation right away.   She could not move until the high tide came.   She was marooned upon the rock on which she rested.

She was in angry mood—angry because I had discovered her, and she was frightened too!

It is all very difficult to describe, but she was the size of an ordinary young human being, with the same features; but she had an *arched* back. She was very beautiful—ravishingly so!

For minutes only, the mermaid and I gazed at one another; then realising that what I saw was supernormal, I took to my heels in terror. What I had seen, coupled with the remembrance of my dog's howls on

PLATE XI

The late Alexander Gunn, Balchreick, Kinlochbervie
Sutherland

reaching the shore, frightened me, and I must confess I followed after my dog in trembling fear of the maiden of the sea.

You may all scoff at me as much as you choose and attribute this story to drink, if you will. But I *saw* a real mermaid off *Ruadh an Fhir Leithe*, and I will not depart from my story for any man on earth. If only my dog were alive to-day he would corroborate my story in his own canine language. What I saw was *real*; I actually encountered a mermaid.

Alexander Gunn, a highly respected small land-holder on the Kinlochbervie Estate, died in December 1944.

Mermaids at Sheigra and Loch Inchard

Not very long ago, two girls who were walking along the shore near Sheigra, a little way south of Ruadh an Fhir Leithe, declared that they had both seen a mermaid (which corresponded exactly to the description of the one seen by Mr. Gunn in 1900) slip gracefully off a rock into the sea at Na Stacain.

On Saturday, June 24th, 1939, while fishing from a rowing-boat in Loch Inchard, a lady staying at Garbet Hotel, Kinlochbervie, suddenly noticed what she took at first to be a bunch of yellow seaweed rise to the surface of the water a few feet in front of her, while the boat she was in was peacefully drifting off Achriesgill Bay. To her surprise, the " sea tangle " turned round in the water, revealing a beautiful face! It was not seaweed at all, but fair golden hair out of which peered a lovely face with blue eyes and delicate colouring.

The lady in the rowing-boat was tongue-tied with astonishment, and when she finally managed to direct her friends attention to the object in the water, the mermaid sank from view, and her tail broke the surface of the water before she disappeared into the inky depths.

When the lady mentioned the matter later to her ghillie, he told her that this mermaid had often been seen floating in Loch Inchard, or lying on the rocks by the shore. She had never spoken to anyone, and never done anyone any harm, but for all that, the local people were afraid of her as something " not canny ".

A Kinlochbervie Merman

For sheer bleakness and desolation, the district immediately south of Cape Wrath cannot be beaten. The hills lie piled in aloof majesty above the sea; lonely sea-water lochs wind their way into the land, with perhaps one shepherd's cottage in hundreds of square miles.   Here are only the winds and the waves, and the reflections of the brooding hills.   It is " a haunted place with a timeless mystery all its own ".

It was amid surroundings such as these that Mr. John Falconer and two fishermen friends encountered the merman. They were rowing their boat past Creig Mhòr, close into the shore, when an unearthly figure rose suddenly to the surface of the water, and stuck up out of the sea to its waist some distance from their boat.*   It was a grotesquely hairy, semi-human figure, and its expression was evil.   It had beady black eyes, and there was a diabolical grin on its face.   When the three men saw a powerful tail under the water, they knew that they were looking at a merman.

This horrible figure remained gazing at them with an expression of diabolical malevolence, then, as suddenly as it had appeared, it sank into the mysterious depths before their eyes.

They never rowed the boat harder for shore than they did that evening.

Mr. Falconer insisted that what he and his friends encountered was none other than a merman.   He had sailed most of the Seven Seas and had encountered many strange sea-creatures and the nearest approach to the creature sighted off Creig Mhòr was the aquatic mammal known as the dugong which he had encountered in the Red Sea.   This animal had a bilobate tail like a whale's, and is the only animal known to graze at the bottom of the sea.   " But," said our narrator, " as the Dugong is found only in the Red Sea, it must have taken a very long holiday to reach the Kinlochbervie coast."

* Seals occasionally lift themselves perpendicularly out of the water exposing half their bodies and look as like the representation of a mermaid as possible. The wild and mournful cry of the seal is difficult to describe—something between the mew of a cat and the howl of a dog in distress—a weird and unpleasant sound which harmonises with the wild scenery of their surroundings.   Highlanders are by no means prepossessed in favour of the good looks of a seal or " sealgh " as they term it.   " You are a sealgh " is an expression of disgust which, when uttered by one crofter to another, is considered a great insult and a climax to every known term of reproach.

Whether merman or not, what the three men saw was a foul thing. Two of the fishermen died shortly afterwards, of peculiar maladies, aggravated by the memory of their frightful encounter; and John Falconer alone remains alive to tell the tale.

Sandwood Cottage

Sandwood Cottage is perhaps the most remote and solitary inhabited dwelling in the whole of Scotland, being situated amid bleak and desolate surroundings on the south side of Sandwood Loch, roughly nine miles south of Cape Wrath and about one mile east of the haunted beach of Sandwood. On the north side of Loch Sandwood there is only one shepherd's cottage (also reputed to be haunted) within 60,000 acres of land.

Nearby are the remains of the ruined homesteads of the last of the Mackays of Sandwood.

According to Mr. Gunn: " I had been at the sheep all day, and decided to sleep in Sandwood Cottage overnight. I entered the cottage as dusk was falling, and after making myself a cup of tea, I locked and bolted the front door and went upstairs to the room above the kitchen, took off my clothes, extinguished the candle, and went to bed.

" Just as I was going to sleep, I heard steps—distinct footfalls padding about below. I got out of bed and put my ear to my bedroom door and heard footfalls going from room to room downstairs. I said to myself, ' that's queer, for I bolted the door; surely I must have locked someone into the house who entered before I did—but who on earth would be seen near Sandwood of all places at this time of night? '

"As the tramp, tramp, tramp continued, I dressed myself, and with candle in hand I opened my bedroom door and descended the stairs.

" I carefully searched every room in the house, but found nothing. I went back to bed again and heard no more that night."

Mr. Gunn was perfectly convinced that there was no living creature—human or animal—with him in the cottage that night. His explanation of the ghostly footsteps was an interesting one:

Some years before, a wealthy tourist had come all the way from Australia to see Sandwood Cottage, as he had heard of it as a suitable place at which to stay while fishing Sandwood Loch. He fell completely under the spell of the desolate countryside, which called him back again and again. He had visited the cottage on three separate occasions, and was each time more loth to leave.

The local people had learnt with regret of his death in Australia shortly after his last sojourn among them. To the haunting cry of Sandwood, " *C'uin a thig thu rithist?* " (when will you come again?)—the dying man had answered, " *Cha'n fhada gu sin* " (it will not be long). He had returned in spirit to visit his spiritual home.

All houses wherein men have lived and died are haunted houses

LONGFELLOW.

PLATE XII

Stoer Bay, Sutherland

CHAPTER XVIII

ENCOUNTER WITH A SEA MONSTER OFF CLACHTOLL

by R. MACDONALD ROBERTSON

" The seamew's lonely laughter
Flits down the flowing wave,
The green scarts* follow after
The Surge where cross-tides rave."

" I saw the monsters . . . go heaving by; the long lithe beasts
that are toothed to their tails."

JAMES STEPHENS

Towards the end of June 1938, while fishing for haddock
and cod, etc., from a fairly large rowing-boat, as the
summer sun was on the descendent, over the sand bank
in the beautiful Bay of Clachtoll (Stoer, Sutherland)—roughly
two miles out to sea, due west of the ancient Broch of Clachtoll
—I, in company with two men (one the local deer-fencer of
the district) and two ladies had a most remarkable " take "
on sea rods and hand lines.

Prior to setting out in the boat, we had spent that afternoon
spearing flounders which remained at low tide in the pools
and runs in the sheltered little sandy bay. By wading where
the placid water was a foot or two in depth, we had obtained
with the assistance of long light spears, a good basket of fish.
When a flounder is taken out of water and laid on the sand,
by a peculiar lateral motion of the fins the fish tries to bury
itself as quickly as if he is still in his own element. During
this operation, we were amazed at the number of rabbits on
the hillside, on the arm of the sea. The rabbits which inhabit

* Cormorants or shags

the sand hills are certainly heavier and larger than those living in a more cultivated country, notwithstanding that their food consists almost entirely of fine grass and dry bent, with the variety of a little sea-weed. Small patches of bright emerald-coloured velvety-looking grass grow here and there on the corners of ground formed by the debris of the cliffs.

On our way seaward we trailed, with rods in hand, our lines behind the boat baited alternatively with white, yellow and red sea-flies. The mackerel, saith, gurnet and lithe darted periodically, and with true aim at the flies, when close to the boat as eagerly as when at some distance, and fought most powerfully; but there was always the danger while rowing close inshore, of the bottom of our boat staving in on some hidden rocks, round which the large tangle floated gracefully in the swell of the wavelets, which concealed the rocks from which they grew.

As we made our way to the fishing ground out at sea, the wind had almost dropped entirely. It was an exceptionally fine evening as we rowed westward in the singularly pure and clear atmosphere.

On looking back, were the great giants of the Stack forest. Nowhere is there a finer view of this mighty ring of mountains and nothing can exceed the scene as one gazes towards the varied line of abrupt rocks surmounted by the dark mountains in the background. A confusion of rock and stone—mountains which appear as if they had been splintered and broken up by some great convulsion of the earth. The entire coast here is very grand and steep, exposed to the whole force of the ocean; the rocks are cut up and weather-beaten to a degree unknown in more southern or more sheltered counties. To the west the view of Lewis is very fine, while looking inland rise the strangely formed mountains of Suilven, Bracbag, Ben More, Canisp, Culmore, Quinag, Coulbeg, Glasven, Stack Polly, Ben Leod and Ben Hee which stand out in most impressive grandeur, unlike any others in the British Isles, giving a grand character of scenery wherever they appear.

On arriving at the sand-bank, we baited with mussels which we had previously procured from Loch Laxford—very

As we saw them on 20 June 1953 on a never to be forgotten afternoon from above the "maidens loch" during our holiday at mrs mackenzies, Cacarragh Clachtoll Stoer.

PLATE XIII

The Hump-Back of Suilven from the " Grey Castle," Sutherland

large shells! We used single " round bend " hooks mounted on wire traces; strong tackle which can hold almost anything! The sea here is of considerable depth, but so clear that shells or any white objects can be seen forty to fifty feet from the surface. Every time, before our baits reached the bottom, we had a " nibble ", and we literally filled our boat with white fish of all descriptions including whiting, codling, haddock, plaice, etc., many of which exceeded several pounds in weight. I have never before witnessed such a splendid catch! In fact I could hardly have imagined that there could ever have been so many greedy fish in one particular part of the sea, nor of so heavy a variety.

It was now high tide. It was a sublime evening and everything was stillness and the sea was almost as placid as a mill-pond, as our craft gently rose and fell to the rhythm of the Atlantic swell.

Great sharks, their black back fins erect and moving about slowly, periodically disported themselves above the surface of the water. We had our rifles loaded in readiness, but they kept their distance.

My wife who was using a hand line, suddenly informed us that her hook had fouled. " Pull it straight up," said our skipper, " you must have struck something imbedded in the bottom." She pulled and pulled and hauled; but with no effect. I thought for some time that she was foul of a rock; but when something stirred at last, in answer to her resolute tugging, it seemed as if she had dislodged some heavy inanimate object. Then suddenly she felt a quiver and, on handing the line over to me, I felt a dead weight, as if an anchor had been entangled on the paternoster. As I, in turn, handed her my rod, I sensed a peculiar vibration on the end of the line—the tremor of a large creature. " It is a fish! " I shouted. The boatman said: " Then go easy with him and pull him to the surface " (in Gaelic). I replied, " I cannot, I am unable to move him, besides he is too far down." Then a tussle royal ensued; but I held on like grim death. How the wretch pulled! His volunteer efforts gradually began to haul the boat slowly through the water.

I

Away went the fish at considerable speed. I played out yard after yard of line—yard after yard, until all my length of cord was exhausted! Even then, did this monster continue upon its course. I grasped the end of the line as well as I could, from over the prow of the boat, which seemed periodically to go down under the strain. Still holding on to the cord, which almost cut my fingers to the bone, I shouted to our ghillie for assistance. By this time the boat was beginning to head right out to sea in the direction of Lewis, pulled by the under-water beast, but I still clutched hold of the last strand of line which was knotted on to a wooded rectangular piece of wood.

By this time our boat had developed the wake of a miniature destroyer and was travelling through the wavelets out to sea, and every now and then the nose of the vessel dipped down in the sea; but I still held on.

" Donald Dubh! " swore our ghillie, in his best Gaelic, " you have caught the very Devil himself; if you don't let go we shall all perish! " But I still grasped hold of the line while our boat ploughed through the waves in a direct line for Stornoway! " Nonsense," said I, " I'll play him silly."

For several hundred yards, I should say, we were hauled through the waves at alarming speed; then the ladies got frightened, likewise our ghillie, who, coming forward, took out his gralloching knife, and before I could stop him, he cut the string! Naturally, I was very cross with him; but perhaps his prompt action saved our lives, as by this time the boat was beginning to fill up with water and we had forgotten the bailer, which was an old tin pot.

Although I did not divulge my emotions outwardly, I actually rejoiced inwardly when the length of line parted.

Suddenly the scene changed. The wind grew ice-cold and started to blow great guns.

We were under way in a minute, making headway for the shore, when the full weight of the storm fell upon us with unexpected fury. I was astonished at the sudden change in the weather. Thunder rumbled in the distance, and great black clouds gathered on the horizon and I sensed a sinister foreboding as the rain-drops stung me in the face.

In no time, white horses were rolling up the bay and the gale seemed to be gaining strength as the Ross-shire and Sutherland peaks loomed up in the distance in dark profile. Mountain gloom and mountain glory appeared as if they had fallen down from the Heavens, having little to do with the country or each other either in shape, material, position or character.

The difficulty which now confronted us was the problem of making for the shore; for already a high sea was running and the boat was fast filling with water due to the waves washing over the bows, while the craft was rocking to and fro as the waves lapped its sides. At the same time, I judged by the expression on the faces of my friends that they were somewhat anxious about our journey back to the anchorage.

Battling with the wind and rain in our endeavours to pull our way against the now strong breeze was no easy task, and at times we made little or no progress against the waves which frequently lashed over the side of the boat; but we took turn about at rowing, keeping the heavy haddock boat head on to the ever-increasing wind. In fact, we almost despaired as the breeze and lashing rain caught us amidship on occasions, as we struggled up the middle of this sea water loch in the teeth of the elements. By this time the gale was blowing so hard and the seas were running so high, that our craft rose and fell, pitched and rolled and tossed about like a cork on the ocean. Time and distance were in our minds obliterated, like a trance, for the sea was becoming wilder every moment, while the rain drenched us to the skin as our oars bent and creaked under the strain.

The hills in front of us seemed like an unbroken barrier of frowning demons barring our course through the storm in fantastic outline.

The squall now seemed to be blowing down the coast from a south-easterly direction in a perfect hurricane right from the shore which we had left some time ago. Owing to the lowness of the stern, our only chance of safety was to keep the head of the fishing-boat to windward, a matter of no small difficulty, as the wind blew in the most violent gusts and increased every moment. The slightest turn of the boat, which would bring her at all broadside to the wind, must have instantly swamped her.

The fearful run was happily a short one, and finally our boat drove into the ooze and weed, which are thickest at the bend of the bay. We trundled out into the shallow water and after an unpleasant wade through the pounding surf, reached dry land, feeling very fatigued. According to our ghillie, had it not been for the extra ballast, due to the weight of our catch of fish lying amongst our feet, the boat might have turned bodily over by the fury of that south-easterly bluster!

Having landed, wet through, we were very glad to look back at the water which was white with foam. Nothing but a strong arm and good rowing saved us from certain drowning, which would nevertheless have been our fate had anything given way about the oars or pins they worked upon.

Should any of my readers find himself on a hot close day, sea fishing off Clachtoll Bay, let him not forget—as on that occasion we did—to keep a sharp lookout to seaward, and if he should notice a dark yellow haze forming in the offing towards the south-west, let him lose no time in making for the shore. The fury and suddenness of the chill wind which follows that warning-appearance, can hardly be exaggerated. Fortunately it eventuates but rarely, generally after a long spell of hot dry summer weather.

I think the high education of British *Salmonidae*, coupled with the growing demand for fly fishing, has given increased importance to every detail of lures required for successful sport on rivers and lochs. In a sea battle, however, one is not embarrassed with any special nicety of equipment, for when a monster takes to pulling a boat, a length of coarse tackle serves as a tow-rope.

In view of the foregoing, I have come to the conclusion that the heavy sea creature which we hooked off Clachtoll, might have been a species of large skate (*Rara Vulgaris*) or

Ray; but again, the skate is a comparatively slow moving creature. Skates and rays about our coasts number upwards of a dozen species. So-called Devil-fishes of warmer waters than ours belong to this group—known as Eagle-Rays (15 feet long)—lash out with their muscular lissom tails, all barbed with spines from which a rank poison is said to exude.

Torpedo Rays—British specimens have slight power to give electric shocks. They weigh seventy to eighty pounds, and possess a natural electric battery. They are not only known to stun fish with a flick of their tails, but to kill and swallow a six-pound salmon as well. The skate is nothing more than a highly specialised shark by virtue of the fact that it has, through generations, transferred its seat of locomotion from the tail to the pectoral fins. These have become enormously developed at the expense of the tail, which has become greatly reduced in size and functions only as a rudder. The species are found all round the coast of Europe. The cunning of the skate is well known. It is a cousin of the shark; but the shark is, what may be termed, a round fish, moving swiftly by virtue of a side-to-side scuttling action of the tail, whilst the skate may be properly called a " flat " fish. Its change has been brought about by the enormous development of the pectoral fins which form huge fleshy lobes on each side of the body—fins that supersede the tail and propel the body by a series of movements resembling the lateral fins of the plaice or sole. Had the monster we hooked been a shark, in all probability it would have shown itself on the surface of the water—hence my theory that the creature *may* have been a large skate; but nevertheless, there are many strange fish in the sea. So the matter remains one of doubt.

While on the subject of sea monsters, it is interesting to note that Aldrovandus, a Bologna naturalist, at the height of the Renaissance, wrote a treatise on monsters, while Ambrose Pare, surgeon to King Henry III of France, was no less credulous and contributed works on sirens and men-at-arms of the sea, all covered with scales. From writings of Olans Magnus, our modern authors have not only detailed the horrors of the sea-serpent but have illustrated the creature issuing

CETACEAN ATTACKING A SHIP
Fascimile from the *De Gentibus Septentrionalibus*, 1555, by Olans Magnus

from the breakers and hurling itself bodily upon ships in
order to devour the crews.*

The Bishops of Uppsala represent Catacca whose formidable
jaws crush boats and Buffon. They describe cuttle-fish (or
Polypus), in the northern seas, of such dimensions, that a whale
is a pigmy in comparison to them; such cuttle-fish he contri-
butes, are of such prodigious size that, when they rest motionless
half out of the water, their bodies covered with sea weeds,
have, on occasions, been mistaken for islands floating on the
surface of the waves and sailors have been known to anchor
their ships on the flanks of these sea monsters to land on their
backs. According to Olans Magnus, fishermen are known
to have cooked a meal at a glowing fire lighted on the body
of one of these fantastic creatures.

Dennis de Montfort describes cuttle-fish which, by means

* The old Scandinavian writers attribute to the sea-serpent a length of six
hundred feet, with a head closely resembling that of a horse, black eyes, and a
kind of white mane. According to them, it is only met with in the ocean, where
it suddenly rears itself up like a mast of a ship of the line, and gives vent to hissing
noises which appal the hearer, like a tempest roar. The Norwegian poets compare its progress to the flight of a swift arrow. When the fishermen descry it
they row in the direction of the sun, the monster being unable to see the mwhen
its head is turned towards that planet. They say that it revolves sometimes in
a circle around the doomed vessel, whose crew thus find themselves assailed on
every side.—*The Mysteries of the Ocean*, by Mangin—Tr.

of their immense arms thickly covered with suckers, have been known to encircle ships and wreck them by plunging them into the depths, and attributes the inexplicable disappearance of some boats to these mighty Denizens of the Ocean. Such monsters are said to possess gleaming eyes and even twine their hideous arms round masts of ships-of-war which they tightly strain.

To think of monsters in our civilised world to-day, is like stepping back through the centuries. Stories of them have drifted down to us on the ocean of time, their strangeness bringing to our minds a dream and a picture of that unknown world immediately far removed, where man was lost.

An unexpected *rencontre* with a big fish from a rowing boat, even when attended to with no danger, is generally the reverse of pleasant, when it tows the craft about for an indefinite space of time.

And so rests another unsolved mystery at the instance of a denizen of the deep.

In conclusion, if I have dwelt on my subject with too much detail or in too laudatory a spirit, I ask my readers' indulgence.

SEA SERPENT
Facsimile from the *De Gentibus Septentrionalibus*, 1555, by Olans Magnus

CHAPTER XIX

THE ROAD TO KYLESKU

by R. MACDONALD ROBERTSON

IN THIS excursion to remoter Sutherland, of which I offer a
few notes, my object was to break away for a few days from
the cares of business.

Feeling that I merited a change of air, and being envious
of friends who had already left town on holiday, I decided to
follow their example one late evening towards the end of the
month of May.

I may say that the happiest days of my life have been
spent roaming about the bens and glens of our Scottish
Highlands, mixing with the local people and listening to their
soft Gaelic speech.

Late that evening I left Edinburgh with my wife and our
constant companion, the bull-terrier. Yes, we had suddenly
decided to journey to north-west Sutherland, sleeping in shifts
in the old car.

The urge to revisit Kylesku had suddenly taken possession
of us, and in no time we were speeding northwards through
the spring night air.

Night motoring has a distinct fascination of its own,
coupled with a sense of mystery and, even in the dark, the
Highlands of Scotland possess a weird fascination. As the
poet wrote:

> Bright and fierce and fickle is the south,
> But dark and true and tender is the north.

and the land as well as its people bids every traveller *Ceud
mile failte* (a hundred thousand welcomes). At night-time,
things look queerly strange and objects take weird shapes as
the darkness falls upon the fleeting landscape.

To each of us the Scottish Highlands conjure up a different

picture. Some may think of the pine woods and the rushing rivers of Perthshire, with its ancient castles and stately mansions others of the farm steadings and the fragrant meadows of the Black Isle. Still others will visualise the treeless plains of Caithness or all the romance and beauty of the Western Isles; but to me " The Highlands " mean first and foremost that part of north-west Sutherland, south of Cape Wrath, where lonely sea lochs gleam in the sunlight and the hills lie piled up in aloof majesty above the noise of the breakers; far ahead of the more conventional " beauty spots " of the Trossachs and elsewhere:

> Land of brown heath and shaggy wood
> Land of the mountain and the flood

where nearly every place has a legend attached to it.

On reaching the outskirts of Inverness, there was a clear sky with scarcely a suspicion of cloud, and on the horizon, peak after peak on the mountains ahead of us caught the first rays of the rising sun. The freshness of the morning air rendered exhilaration and our enthusiasm seemed to communicate itself to each other without words.

After leaving Inverness, we headed northward. Dingwall and Strathpeffer alone have a host of fishing stories; but I am informed that quite recently a very large brown trout was captured by a local lad (fishing with worm) at the mouth of the Peffery Burn, where it enters the Cromarty Firth, which weighed some 4 lbs.

On reaching Invergordon, we of course visited old friends who entertained us royally and from whom we heard many amusing yarns, three of which, I think, are worthy of recording.

A Highland minister, after conducting his morning service, took a quiet stroll one summer afternoon by the side of the River Glass. Being thoroughly shocked on observing a wee laddie casting from off the river bank, he went up to him and said: " My child, knowest thou what thou art doing? " " Fishing," replied the youth. " Do you know that you are committing a grave sin by fishing on the Sabbath Day? " said the clergyman. " No," retorted the boy. " Do you know, my dear child, that you will be burnt in Hell fire for this offence? "

But the wee laddie said that he had never heard about this before. " Do you realise that the Lord is watching all your movements—everything you do ? " continued the minister. " No," said the youth, " I never knew this before." " Yes," replied the padre, " He is watching you at the present time casting with that very rod." But the boy merely confessed his entire ignorance about the whole thing. As the minister kept on pressing his point, the youth turned to him and said: " Do you think, sir, the Lord is watching my uncle in Ireland, for he fishes a river like this every Sunday over there? " "Ah, shame be upon him," replied his reverence, " of course He is likewise watching your uncle breaking the Sabbath Day over there and he too, verily, will be consumed for his actions in the burning lake." Thereupon the youth retorted: " Well, all I can say, sir, is that there must be some mistake somewhere, as I don't possess any uncle in Ireland at all! "

An angler inquired from his ghillie whether there were many fish in the River Conon. " If you were to boil the water you take out of it," replied the ghillie, " you'd be getting the taste of salmon in your tea! "

Another Highland minister had just preached a fervent sermon on social evils to a local congregation and, winding up his discourse, he said on the subject of alcohol: " If I had anything to do with whisky, rum or beer or any other intoxicating drink, I should have the whole lot poured down the Alness water." At the conclusion of the service, the closing hymn was announced: " Shall we gather at the river! "

Highlanders, as a race, have a great and noble heritage to live up to. As the Rev. Hon. Ian Macpherson said on one occasion: " I am proud of this land of heroes, of glens, of straths, of mists and of gloom. I believe that there is a great future for it. The world has gone through a great cataclysm, but above it all stands the solemn dignity of our native Highlands. It is the duty of all of us, in whatever sphere of public or private life we may be, to remember the greatness of our past, to remember those hills and to teach our children their dignity and their grandeur. It is the duty of all of us here to help this native land of ours."

And so on our journey we continued and after crossing the picturesque old bridge over the River Shin we halted at the Inveran Hotel where our good friend Angus Macpherson and his wife gave us a great welcome.

How I wish there were more old-time Inns like Inveran, where the landlord receives his guests with jolly countenance and dignified hearty feelings, instead of leaving them to the care of servants. In old days, the Highland landlord *was the Inn.* Alas, now-a-days, feeling and simplicity are rapidly giving place to artificial appearance and pretence in palatial modern hotel atmosphere with swaggering tourist guests.

After being shown to our bedroom which overlooked the River Shin, we partook of a sumptuous supper in the delightful little old-fashioned dining room in which burned a cheerful peat fire. During our meal we were entertained by our host on the pipes some distance from without. No one can possibly judge the bagpipes unless he has been familiar with the sound of the piobaireachd in its native element. "As naturally as the curlew to the shore or grouse to the moor or the seal to the sea, so naturally belong the bagpipes to the open air."

After a pleasant conversation with some friends, we retired for the night to be peacefully lulled to sleep by the sweet voice of the river with its deep toned murmurings, " a slumbrous sound—a sound that brings the feelings of a dream."

I wakened early to the shrill clarion of a cockerel, when my dog gave me his usual prompt signal hinting that it was time to be up and ready for our usual morning stroll. There had been a heavy rainfall during the night, which made it cooler in the morning, although the sun was shining.

I could not resist the sudden impulse to cast a line before breakfast, so dressing hurriedly, I assembled my rod and made straightway down the River Shin to where it enters the Kyle. To start with, I selected a cast comprising a " Silver Wilkinson " and a " Peter Ross " and almost with my first cast I hooked and landed a goodly sea trout of about 2 lbs. which put up a grand fight. As the tide was ebbing fast, sooner than lose an opportunity of exhausting this part of the Kyle before the tide should turn, I made my way up-stream along the bank about a quarter of a mile westward, and commenced to cast downstream from a point where the water takes a gradual turn at the bottom of a field in which a wild swan had its nest.

The turn of the salt water brings up aquatic insects and perhaps small fish; and salmon and sea trout know this and search for food at a time when it is likely to be found. I fail to believe that they can be on the lookout for flies for these are rarely on the surface of the water. I imagine that they mistake the gaudy fly for a small fish. A sort of imperfect memory of their early food; but flies form a great part of the food of salmon fry and in returning to fresh water they naturally search for their food at the surface.

Wading in from the bank until the water gently lapped the fringe of my kilt, I continued operations by casting at an angle out towards the centre of the tidal water of the River Oykell. Wading in one's shoes and stockings may be considered by many persons a questionable propriety; but in summer months when our rivers are comparatively warm, wading may be practised with little risk to general health. Such a footbath has a certain benefit as it diminishes fatigue and makes the exercise more agreeable besides being an excellent remedy for corns. Gumboots or other wading footwear on the other hand are intolerably clumsy things at their best and are very heating and wearying.

Apart from one or two deep holes, the Kyle is easily waded from this point to where the River Shin discharges itself into it. Without exaggeration, at nearly every third bob of my line, I sensed an offer; but on many occasions the fish came short, until finally, after several attempts, I was fast into a large yellow trout which after playing, I successfully brought to net. It weighed just under three pounds.

By the time I exhausted the beat, I had accounted for another brown trout of smaller weight, as also seven beautiful sea trout most of which fell to a " Grouse and Green ", and returned back to the hotel, in good time for breakfast, with a heavy creel.

It was fine to be once again in contact with mother nature,

away from the cares and worry of the city, with its artificial life, where many dare not be what they actually are, but are always anxiously striving to appear as belonging to some other order of humanity. Solitude is a consoler to the mind and invigorates the whole system. It gives one time to postulate and enjoy the beauties of nature.

After leaving Inveran, we passed through the wooded hamlet of Rosehall (a stately progeny of pines, with all their floating foliage, richly robed) to which point the tide flows a distance of some twelve miles from Bonar Bridge. Strath Oykell forms the boundary between the shires of Ross and Sutherland. Shortly afterwards, we reached the River Cassley, an excellent angling stream with a remarkable waterfall about a mile above the bridge, forming a salmon leap.

Skirting Castle-na-Coir on the Sutherland side of the Oykell, the road branches westwards along the banks of the river with its many graceful windings as far as the township of Brae with Tutimtarbhach its ancient burial ground.

Between Brae and Oykell Bridge, the hills appeared more barren and rugged with red heather intermixed with deers' hair moss, relieved by occasional clumps of birch. There is a formidable looking waterfall near Oykell Bridge Hotel, in the " pot " below which many a good salmon was frequently taken in the bag-net in olden days. The Oykell Bridge Hotel is another of those very homely and comfortable Inns with an old-fashioned atmosphere about it, and the inn-keeper personally sees to the comfort of his hotel guests.

Climbing the moorland hill, we caught the first view of the lofty mountain of Canisp, distinguished by its sharp conical shape.

A short way past Lubcroy, the whole aspect seemed strangely to change as we pulled up to admire the soul-stirring scenery.

A little farther on we were particularly impressed with the sudden and unexpected appearance of several strange looking chocolate-coloured lofty conical shaped mountains, quite detached from each other—three in particular, Culmore in Coigach to the south, Suilven with its forked head and hanging side in the centre, and Canisp on the north.   As we proceeded, other peaks came into sight including Ben More, Culbeg, and Stack Polly, unlike any others in the British Isles.

Ten miles on our journey from Oykell Bridge, we reached Loch Borrolan into which flows the Altnacealgach Burn—the boundary between Ross and Sutherland in this district.

There are a number of theories regarding the derivation of the name Altnacealgach; but I think that it is now universally agreed that the word signifies " the burn of deceivers " or " Cheat Burn " on account of a dispute which arose in determining the boundary between the two counties, some witnesses having sworn that they were standing in Ross-shire ground because they had filled their boots with Balnagown earth.

Awheel again, we passed Ledmore.   The road here inclines to the north and while the surface of the land appears to decline to that direction, the Ledbeg burn on the left hand flows towards the south, giving to a stranger the anomalous impression that the stream forces its way up against the ascent.

At Ledmore a path branches off to the scattered little village of Elphin on the south-west, on the road to Ullapool, some sixteen miles distant.

One of the most successful fishing holidays I have ever spent was in 1937 when I resided for over a week at a croft at Knockan, where I accounted for *heavy* baskets.

Skirting Loch Awe to the west, with its small wooded islets, we soon came in sight of the upper end of Loch Assynt. On our right, many noisy burns brawled down the hillside. The springs of Assynt are recognised for their purity and size, the water being ice-cold even in the heat of summer.

Shortly after passing the farm of Stronchrubie, we ran over and killed a large female adder crossing the road.   These poisonous vipers are very common in this part of the country. Not so long ago, several men engaged in repairing the fence round Assynt Lodge, being so alarmed at the number of snakes, found it necessary to tie down the bottom of their trousers to the top of their boots to avoid being bitten by these reptiles.   The adder is the only dangerous snake we have in Britain; but its bite can prove fatal if the wound is not timeously attended to. The application of neat whisky to the affected part is a good antidote, I am told; perhaps, hence the attraction for spending a fishing holiday in the district!

Descending into the valley along the base of a range of rugged mountains, we arrived in time for tea at Inchnadamph Hotel, surrounded on all sides by very imposing peaks, with the beautiful expanse of Loch Assynt lying ahead of us on the west and the singular mass of Quinag on the north, with the summit of Camisbhe rising high above on the south, in an atmosphere of restful solitude so characteristic of the central wilds of Sutherland.

Inchnadamph stands on a gentle slope between the Loanan and the Traygall burns, both of which flow into the head of Loch Assynt. It lies at the base of the buttress of Ben More, the loftiest mountain in the County. Many years ago, a fishing hatchery was set up at Inchnadamph, and many fine Loch Leven and other trout, I am informed, were liberated in Loch Awe and in the Loanan burn, but this hatchery is no longer in existence.

May I recommend my readers to refer to a small but very interesting booklet (now unfortunately hard to procure) entitled: *Angler's and Sketcher's Guide to Sutherland* by Archibald Young, Advocate (Wm. Paterson, Edinburgh, 1881) which contains very valuable information concerning the County. The author gives some excellent tips concerning angling in the Assynt district.

There can be no doubt, whatsoever, that the lochs in and around this particular part of the County (natural ones) contain specimens of *salmo ferox* far ahead of those caught anywhere else in Scotland; only they tend to have rather fierce-looking heads with formidable rows of teeth, the head being somewhat disproportionally large in proportion to the size of the body. *Ferox* up to 20 lbs. are not uncommon in the district. Local people often catch large specimens on " set-lines " over night. By doing so they actually perform good deeds, in as much as that they help to rid the local water of murderers of hundreds of younger and smaller fish. Sutherland is said to be the one county in Scotland which is free from the *Pike* menace and, in this connection, I refer to my chapter entitled "Angling for Pike " contained in this book.

Shortly after leaving Inchnadamph we headed right, in a due northerly direction, and at Skaig Bridge we commenced the uphill journey to Kylesku. It is a very steep ascent, through a confusion of rock and stone for upwards of several miles. The boulders on either side appear to have been broken up and splintered by some great convulsion of earth, in a succession of wild and rocky passes, confused and disorderly.

Up we went, following our narrow gravelly pathway, with grass and heather growing in the centre of it, until we finally reached the summit. The scenery was wild and dreary and it became even more so, as we descended the rough mountain road.

It is very difficult to describe in detail this unique road to Kylesku. The only solution is that, if you are to appreciate it, you must make the journey yourself.

On reaching the bridge which spans the Alt na Branhan, we pulled up at the side of the road in order to photograph the waterfall which drops some one hundred and fifty feet sheer out of Loch-na-Gainmhich forming this burn. We did so by leaving the high-road after walking up the bed of a very uneven brawling stream. This waterfall is very awe-inspiring, and when in full volume, commands one the finest and fiercest cataracts in the district. We cast a line, fishing worm in this burn, with amazing result, and in no time returned to our car with about ten fine brown trout caught within the space of twenty-five minutes. Scrambling along the banks of this rocky stream is by no means easy.

What delighted us most, was the fragrance of the mountains coming forth to greet us from off the heather.

The only obstacle we encountered on our descent towards Kylesku was a cart with a load of peats lumbering along the narrow winding road. The extent and majesty of the mountain screens on all sides of us were indescribably beautiful and majestic, as mass upon mass of mountains reared themselves up, all seen from different aspects.

PLATE XIV

Kylesku Ferry, Sutherland

On approaching Unapool, we beheld that lovely view of the inlet to the Kyle, as grand a sea loch as can be imagined. Here were patches of cultivation around the few cottages which stud the landscape, and far away on each side extended heathery moorland varying in hue from pale russet to the deepest crimson " clutching the clouds of Heaven "—and thence to the sea.

From this point the road became very rough for the next mile or so; but we felt really enchanted, as we drove down-hill past Lochan-Dubh towards our destination through a fragrant atmosphere of peat reek and bog-myrtle mixed with sea-tangle.

The sun was dipping behind the mountains as we pulled up in front of the little Kylesku Hotel, where we were greeted by our old friend, Mr. Moffat, the Inn-keeper, in true hospitable Highland style.

I shall never forget the heavenly sunset which we beheld that night.

" Into the western sky the sun went down into the haze of a soft bank of cloud. Then Nature, that supreme artist, began her transformation. The sky changed to a soft purple, the hills to an inky blue. The outer Isles blurred and faded, but above them, stretching upwards to Lewis, came a long bar of delicate green. The soft darkness quietly stood there, softening to the caress of approaching night. Then the sun in its blaze of gold and red, transformed the upper clouds into masses of golden light. Mass upon mass of light cloud was permeated with ethereal fire. Is it any wonder that the lonely Gael, beholding all this grandeur, should cherish thoughts of another and finer world? Ah *tir nan og!* Is it any wonder that in the Gael should well up dreams of the land of the ever young? Surely to set sail over the dark waters in the dying sun, softly sailing into the dim West, would bring him to *Tir nan og.* And surely the souls of the dead would gather at the mouth of some ageless glen where the waters of untold centuries lapped gently on the shingle, there to await the coming of twilight, before setting out on their last journey to the Land of Eternal Youth, lying over the dim waters."

K

CHAPTER XX

KYLESKU

by R. MACDONALD ROBERTSON

KYLESKU is a secluded seaside nook on the west coast of Sutherland as a glance at the Ordnance Survey sheet will show. Many tourists pass this little speck without observing anything of interest to arrest attention. They have no " eyes to see "; but I claim sympathy with those who can enter into the spirit of such scenes, and drink deep draughts of natural peace from the mere contemplation of such simple natural landscapes, which present themselves in an endless succession of scenery magnificent and wild.

Identity of tastes, in so far as recreation in the form of angling is concerned, has prompted me to write this article, as nature is more appreciated by those who only occasionally visit the far north-west, than by those whose lot is cast in the very centre of most captivating Highland scenery.

As any attempt by me to draw a pen-picture of Kylesku would fall very short of the mark, I can only suggest that my readers, if they have not yet encountered the mountain glory of this delightful district, will one day do so during their holidays in the north and halt for a brief span at Kylesku Inn to enjoy the peaceful atmosphere of a land which is:

> Silent, beside the never-silent waves,
> At rest, in all this moving up and down.

There are many guide books which ably describe this back o' beyond little haven of rest, but in order to appreciate the true atmosphere, one must visit the place for himself. Before proceeding so far afield, however, my readers would be well advised to make a careful study of *The Gazetteer of Scotland*.

Kylesku Inn is beautifully situated on Loch Glendhu and is surrounded by wild and romantic scenery. The loch

penetrates deeply into this mountainous region, dividing itself
into two branches—Loch Glendhu and Loch Glencoul about
a mile east of the ferry—the former some three miles and the
latter roughly five miles long, surrounded by a ring of towering
mountains of all shapes and sizes, their declivities ending at
the water's edge.

Although comparatively little known, as a fisherman's
dream spot, I go one step further and term it an Angler's
Paradise as there are many almost virgin lochans and burns
(a number of which are nameless) to be put to the test within
an easy radius on both sides of the Kyle; but permission is
required to fish the waters on the north side of the sea loch.
The salt water is at the very door of the hotel, where trolling
for sea trout can be enjoyed as also sea fishing (line or otherwise).
Suffice to say that, without exaggeration, I know of no other
place in Scotland where I have spent so many happy hours
or filled my basket so full of fish of all sorts. Apart from
fishing altogether, this part of the Highlands bristles with
folklore and it makes a most ideal spot for the brush of the
artist.

One delightfully fresh and breezy morning in early summer, we met some friends round the breakfast table at Kylesku
Inn, including the then President of the Edinburgh Association.
We made up a fishing party. Three of us decided to combine
in trying out the Mystery Lochs situated below the mountain
of Quinag, on the Inchnadamph-Drumbeg road, while other
members of the party resolved to fish Lochan Unapool.

We parted just as the sun was beginning to shine brilliantly
from a blue unclouded sky while gulls screamed lazily overhead. After baling the boat, we pushed off from the bank
into an ideal ripple. A small fellow rose boldly to the dropper
and within the space of about a hundred yards from our
starting point, we had several speckled beauties lying on the
floor boards of the boat. The ordinary run of trout in this
loch is about two to the pound, but we had one over $1\frac{1}{4}$ lbs.
in the space of about five minutes on the Red Palmer. We
found that the most productive sport was obtained by casting
near the reeds.

A tapered cast of 2 × gut comprising the usual standard pattern size of Loch Leven flies is all that is necessary for the brown trout lochs in the district; but, if the weather is rough, the Worm-fly with a red or orange tip should be tried.

However, I must not weary my reader with a description of a whole day's fishing, for catching one trout after another, unless there is an exceptional experience to narrate, becomes monotonous.

After lunch, which included a delicious dish of Carrageen Blanc-mange, I decided to visit the rest of our party on the hill lochs, known as " The Mystery Lochs ", so I walked in the direction of Quinag, leaving my wife in company with another angler friend and our ghillie at Lochan-Unapool,

The walk was an exceedingly fatiguing one as the ground was very rough.   Grey rocks protruded from the heather in endless rounded crags and knolls, intersected with burns and peat-mosses and the desolation added no outstanding feature to the undulations.   After about half an hour's hard tramp in a southerly direction, a change came over the scene, as a sudden blast beat down from the mountains ahead and white clouds were hurriedly chasing one another across the sky and by the time I found my friends, who were casting from off the banks on a scattered chain of lochans, the rain had commenced to fall.

I walked from one member of the party to another and found they had all obtained excellent baskets of plump red-spotted trout.

In no time the sky developed a dull leaden outlook and rain was falling in a perpetual drizzle and the scenery was awe-inspiring in the gloomy watery atmosphere.

After partaking of the remains of my sodden sandwiches, I landed a few speckled beauties by wading in from the shore, but as the downpour was showing signs of setting in for the rest of the afternoon, I decided to trudge back to the boat at Lochan-Unapool in order to run my wife back to the hotel.

My friends also decided to beat a hurried retreat to their car which, they informed me, they had left by the side of the Inchnadamph road near the White Bridge.   On leaving them

I never thought of asking where one member of their party had disappeared to. I had taken it for granted that, being an elderly gentleman, he would have, in all probability, seeing the rain coming, fished slowly back to their motor car in order to take shelter.

I was now soaked through to the skin and, on reaching Lochan-Unapool, every indentation in the hillside was transformed into rivulets swelling the little burns into streams. It would be well after 6 p.m. when I found my wife seated in the car, along with my friend and our ghillie, sheltering from the elements, and in no time we were on our way towards the Inn.

Before passing through Newton, we observed in the distance to the west of us, the Unapool burn now coming down in a turbid torrent, so different from its condition the previous evening; but these mountain streams in the district rise very quickly.

While skirting Lochan-Dubh where every gutter in the road was flooded, our ghillie remarked that this small sheet of water was " no good place "; but, as he declined to tell us why, we did not press the point, believing his remark to be connected with the fishing.

On arriving at Kylesku Inn, we decided to await the arrival of the rest of our party for supper.

While waiting in " the Snuggery ", we got into conversation with a most charming young Austrian girl who had just arrived on holiday off the Mail Van. She was clad in easy-walking costume and in perfect English expressed with great delight her feelings on the beauties of Sutherland. She told us she was a University student, that her hobby was mountaineering and that her fiancé from Oxford would be joining her at Kylesku in two days time on their way up to Scourie and thence to Tongue, where they intended to stay in order to climb Ben Loyal.

For over two hours we waited patiently chatting over a refreshment or two; but as there was no sign of our friends, we partook of our evening meal, during which the wind and rain lashed steadily on the window panes.

Supper over, I left the hotel to pay a short visit to an old local friend about half a mile along the road.

It was a wild night as I walked in the direction of his croft and once business matters were discussed and over, I returned to the inn only to find that our friends' car from the hill lochs had come and gone in my absence. One of their fishing party (the elderly gentleman) was missing and could not be found, and the little Austrian girl, who had a good experience of search parties, had returned with them to the chain of hill lochs in order to try to find the unfortunate angler, who might easily have collapsed or met with some misfortune on the mountain side. I thereupon decided to set off likewise to hunt for our missing friend with the bull terrier. It was growing very dark when I, in company with a ghillie, took the car out of the garage; but just as we were commencing our journey in the teeth of the storm, the other car pulled up, and from amidst coils of ropes and tackles (the property of our Austrian friend) out stumbled our lost wanderer in a thoroughly exhausted condition.

Let the story as told, when the Hotel grandfather clock was striking the midnight hour, be a lesson to all anglers who attempt to fish the chain of lochans below Quinag without having in their possession a proper map of the district and a reliable compass.

Our friend from Glasgow in his eagerness to avoid spoiling fishing grounds for his comrades, somehow or other had rambled leisurely by the banks of the mountain tarns, in the direction, as he thought, towards their car, which had been parked by the main road; but instead, owing to the sudden and unexpected change of weather—which had transformed the countryside—he lost his bearing, a very easy thing to do in these parts, and had wandered deeply into the heart of the deer forest completely in the wrong direction where, being utterly confused, he had sunk down in the heather and had given himself up for lost, in the mists which clothed the heights. The wee girl saved his life!

One consolation uppermost in our heart was the fact of viewing on our way upstairs to our bedroom with candles in hand, three large ashets filled with perhaps the finest conditioned brown trout which we had ever set eyes upon; and so ended our first day's angling adventure at Kylesku, a day which we cannot readily forget.

No sooner had I placed my head on the pillow than the wind and rain came on to a degree little short of a tempest. Doors and windows rattled so that sleep was practically out of the question and the very inn trembled to the foundations.

In the morning we enjoyed our catch of trout (fried in oatmeal) for breakfast, and afterwards as the waves were dashing over the jetty pretty freely, I could see how hopeless the conditions were for fishing and decided to remain indoors and wade through some correspondence.

By the time lunch was over, the sky had cleared somewhat, and although the rain was still falling fairly heavily, the wind was gradually abating.

After supper, as the breeze had fallen considerably, I donned my waterproof and wandered up to Loch-an-Dubh for a cast. Loch-an-Dubh is a small pool of water picturesquely situated by the bend of the main road, less than half a mile distant from the hotel. It is surrounded on the south-west side by high dark overhanging rocks, on which cling stunted trees and other foliage and its whole appearance gives a sensation of gloom, even in the best of weather, as it lies in a dark swampy recess encircled by rushes and other vegetation appropriate to marshy bog-land. Owing to the treacherous nature of the spongy banks, there are but few places where one can venture near the water to cast a line, especially in wet weather, as one readily sinks above one's knees in no time. However, as my feet were wet in any event, I did not mind and within the space of about an hour and a half, I managed to land several little black-headed trout on an ordinary standard Loch Leven cast of flies (comprising a Bloody Butcher, a Heckham Peckham and a Red Palmer) which gave me good sport for they were strong fighters.

As the evening began to draw to a close a shiver ran through me, and I sensed a peculiar loneliness coupled with a desire to leave the water and get away from the place to join the lively company of my friends at the Inn. In any event, casting was becoming difficult owing to the fading light. I am not given to let my emotions get the better of me, but I had the peculiar feeling that I was not alone. A queer sort of sensation that I was being watched or followed by someone or something; but putting the whole thing down to a figment of imagination, I walked briskly back to the Inn in the gloaming without encountering a living soul on the way.

After changing my shoes and stockings, I joined my friends round the fire in the sitting room, in the cheery rays of an oil lamp which stood on a table in the middle of the room.

Many good angling yarns were spun that night, before retiring to bed, over some excellent whisky-toddy and tea, which helped to make the evening a thoroughly enjoyable one.

Next morning the wind had subsided, but the rain was still falling and there was a humid freshness in the air. Waterfalls were to be seen in front of us foaming headlong down the bare mountain sides on the north side of the Kyle, carving their silvery way towards the sea, and a great peacefulness reigned amid the mountain gloom of this Highland fastness.

One or two of our friends decided to visit the high cataract at the head of Loch Glen Coul known as Eas-Coul-Aulin while I, having previously obtained permission, resolved to cast a line on Loch-an-Leathail-Bhuain, out of which the Maldie Burn flows into the north side of the Kyle.

Eas-Coul-Aulin is reckoned the highest waterfall in Scotland. It takes place on the stream known as the Amhainn-an-Loch Bhig which tumbles some seven hundred feet in the course of about one and a quarter miles before it empties itself into the head of Loch Beag at the far end of Loch Glen Coul. Below the cascade are some pools on the burn which hold sea trout and numerous brown trout of good average size. Owing to the contour of the land the only feasible way of reaching Eas-Coul-Aulin from Kylesku is by boat; but the upper portion of the fall can be seen taking a precipitous plunge over the Leitir Dubh ridge more than three miles away. On the last occasion on which I visited this cataract, it was in high flood after several days rain and the sight was most striking.

My friend, the local postman, who kindly volunteered to accompany me to the loch, met me at the hotel jetty shortly after breakfast. As the tide was running fairly strong, we had an oar each, but it took us well over an hour before we were able to anchor the boat at the mouth of the Alt Maldie.

Walking a short way from where we anchored, we approached the base of this considerable fall.

It was a very hard uphill trek following the course of the burn past the various cascades on this stream which snarled in angry mood. Climbing upwards was exceedingly stiff work, for we had to force our way knee-deep in places through treacherous peat bog and scramble over slimy boulders along the side of the noisy water which plunged madly down the rocks.

At one part of our journey we were forced to ford the burn in order to gain the higher ground; but we struck the stream at a place where it was broadest, as being the least dangerous course to adopt. The depth was not so great as we anticipated for it was never above our thighs; but the strength of the current, among loose rolling stones repeatedly almost threw us off our feet, in which case the chances were that we should very unceremoniously have been hurried ultimately into the sea as waifs of the finny tribe!

Climbing and wandering among dark recesses have unquestionably all along constituted a marked feature of my idiosyncrasy, and to me there is nothing more exhilarating than the mountain and the view of the distant peaks.

Finally we reached the lower end of the loch, an extensive sheet of water fully two miles long.

As this loch is reckoned to contain large cannibal trout, which cause a lot of damage by preying on their smaller species, we purposely set the " Scantach " before commencing operations with the fly. The " Scantach " is another word for a set-line with about a dozen or so large single round-bend hooks attached to it at intervals of approximately three feet; and after baiting each hook, with a cluster of large earth-worms we sank the whole length of cord under water by means of attaching a heavy stone to each end of it. We set the line purely by way of *experiment* and for no other reason whatever. We had previously been granted permission to do so.

There was a delightful drizzle of rain and the water had that ideal curl on the surface, as we slowly commenced to fish our way up the north-west side of this wild and desolate loch.

As wading a loch gives the angler access to a great area of water and enables him to cast towards fish beyond reach of the bank, fearless of consequences, and undeterred by the lack of waders, we cheerfully entered the water, chancing a future ill in the hope of securing a basket on the fly. And basket we did secure!

After landing several trout of about half a pound weight, a " swashing " rise suddenly caught me unprepared. I struck awkwardly and glimpsed a broad silvery-spotted flank lash the surface. For many minutes I played this fish which leapt several times into the air after rushing about near the bottom. Judging by its antics and the manner in which it fought, I should say it might have weighed anything up to three pounds or more; but suddenly my line went slack and I realised to my dismay, when I reeled in, that the greater part of my cast was gone! Had this fish not caught me off my balance, I should have had him; however, deciding if possible to transact unfinished business with a very superior trout, I affixed a new cast of flies to my line while partaking of a drink of hot coffee and a cigarette, as a golden eagle circled high above us in the distance. An eagle can easily be distinguished even a long way off by the upward tilt of its wing tips, as also by its high speed of flight. Eagles are far more numerous in Sutherland than most people think.

By the time we returned to the *locus* of the " Scantach ", we had filled our bags so full of excellent brown trout (up to 2 lbs.) that we had no available room for more.

On hauling in the " Scantach " we liberated all fish (other than eels) under roughly 1 lb., which were not too badly hooked. While pulling in the final length of cord, a huge brute rushed at a trout already hooked, and notwithstanding its size, seized hold of it, leaving the marks of its teeth on the back and sides of a trout of over $1\frac{3}{4}$ lbs. I only wish I could have had a better view of the " water-kelpie ", as it would appear there can be no limit to the size of the *ferox* in these Sutherland waters, and I must leave my readers to postulate as to the size of a trout which could attempt to devour one of its own species as heavy as the weight above mentioned. I understand brown trout up to 5 lbs. on the fly are not uncommon in this loch, and that one weighing $4\frac{1}{2}$ lbs. was taken last season.

The rain was still falling pretty heavily as we landed back at the pier below the Inn and after mooring the boat we felt the better of a refreshment in the hotel, before changing for our evening meal.

As we had actually more trout than we knew what to do with, I selected about a dozen for dispatch by post to the south and asked my worthy boatman to distribute the remainder among the local people, after the hotel requirements had been satisfied.

During supper it was interesting and gratifying to overhear the impressions which the majesty and wonders of Eas-Coul-Aulin had created in the minds of the various members of the party who had braved the elements in order to make the excursion to the head of Loch Glen Coul to view this fall.

I awoke early next morning to find the sun shining brightly and the whole scene changed. The air had that peculiar salt tang about it, mixed with the fragrant scent of bog-myrtle and peat reek, so fascinating to the nostrils of the man from town, yet how difficult to describe.

I could not resist the temptation of a swim as I looked through my bedroom window on the clear blue dancing water sparkling merrily in front of me; so in company with my dog, made my way to the little bay to the east of the hotel out of reach of the strong current of the Kyle. The water was pretty breathtaking; but actually not quite so chilly as I had expected after the preceding two sunless days. There is nothing like a sea bathe to give one an appetite for breakfast and that morning the porridge and cream seemed to taste better than ever before.

Breakfast over, I took out the gun and, in company with my old friend from Glasgow, who had nearly met his doom by the hill lochs, we wandered leisurely round Cnock an Guaridh behind the Inn where we bagged a few rabbits.

Shortly before lunch-time the sky became overcast and soon the rain began to fall again.   I have often observed that a bright sunny morning in these parts usually ends in rain.

It was quite apparent by the time the mid-day meal was over, that the wet weather had set in for the rest of the day, and as we had arranged to take our departure next morning, we decided to try for a sea trout below the waterfall on the Maldie burn (about three miles from the Ferry) which empties itself into the salt water, on the opposite side near the head of Loch Glen Coul, and as it happened to be the local postman's day off duty, he kindly consented to act as our boatman.

I arranged with a local crofter to dig a quantity of large black-headed worms from his hen run and to cut a number of sinkers from an old piece of lead piping.

Shortly afterwards, while we were in the act of getting our fishing gear ready for the excursion outside the hotel, he rushed up to us in a state of excitement with blood spouting freely from his left hand, clutching a can of worms in his right, saying he had hacked the end off his finger with a knife while cutting sinkers for the fishing.   As luck would have it, a retired Army Doctor, who was also residing at the hotel, happened to come on the scene unexpectedly.   " Quick," he said " give me the end of your finger *at once* before it is too late, and I'll join it together for you."   " Oh, I can't, sir," replied the man, " it is too late."   " Too late," exclaimed the doctor in astonishment, " what do you mean ? "   " Yes, too late it is, sir," retorted the man, " I've given it to the ferret ! "

Once aboard the boat we pushed off and commenced to row with the tide up the loch in the direction of our objective.

Shortly after starting on our voyage to the fall, I affixed a smallish Blue and Silver minnow to a single-strand wire trace on the end of my trolling line.

We had not proceeded very far when our friend at the oars pointed out to us on a little tongue of rock the remains of a

small round dune out of which sprouted a rowan tree, saying
" that is not a canny spot " and, on enquiring why, he explained
that the stones were mingled with human bones of exceptionally
large size.

Just as he was about to tell us the legend, which we gathered
by what he said had some sort of bearing on one concerning
Lochan Dubh, my reel screamed and my rod bent in my hand.
Foot after foot of line raced off the reel through my fingers as
I tried to halt the mad rush of the fish until all of a sudden
there was a hitch in the proceedings, in the form of a mighty
jerk and with dismay, I saw a streak of silver shoot into the
air amid a pearly spray of water, and I realised that my line
had kinked on the reel-drum.   The strain was intense and the
rod bent and pulsated in my hand; but I held on in breathless
excitement expecting any moment to hear the fateful " ping "
such as one hears when a violin string snaps.

By this time our friend at the oars had turned the boat in
the direction from which we had come, to enable me to follow
the fish, which again and again leapt skywards in a fountain
of glittering emeralds before it went down headlong into the
depths.   This gave me a chance to reel in and check the fish
as the strain on the line became less intense on account of its
angle of descent.   But after another wild run for freedom, the
line stopped short once more with a jam, which literally caused
a sort of singing sound.   As good luck, however, would have it,
the fish suddenly altered its course and made straight towards
the boat, and as I was in the act of reeling in as quickly as I
could to avoid any slackness, the reel fell off the rod, on to the
bottom of the boat; but I gripped hold of the line and played
the sea trout as best I could by letting the line slip through
my fingers, putting a strain on it when necessary, until I finally
brought him to netting reach, when my wife made a lunge for
the beast, but missed, and, to my horror, one of the barbs of
the minnow fouled the skirting of the craft.

Throwing down the rod in desperation, I leaned over the
side of the vessel and managed to grip the fish by the gills
and, after wrenching the grapnel free, lifted the kicking mass
of energy on board.   No sooner had I done so than the minnow

fell out of the mouth of the sea trout which weighed just under 4 lbs.

As we proceeded on our way up the Loch, I spent about a quarter of an hour overhauling my line, while our friend from Glasgow attached my trace to his rod and continued to troll the same minnow behind the boat.

In launching a minnow, it is most important to keep the boat moving at a steady pace and to see that the minnow spins easily, before attempting to let out much line, and care should be taken to see that there are no weeds clinging to the hooks, for sea trout will not take a minnow to which weed adheres.

As our friend at the oars pulled us through the water, he kept time to his strokes by chanting delightful Gaelic rowing songs, which seemed to blend harmoniously with the lonely surroundings.

Within the space of about twenty minutes, my Glasgow friend added to my catch another goodly sea trout of about 2 lbs., which put up a terrific struggle before he managed to capture it.

The rain had stopped and the surface of the water was dead calm as we approached our destination—a scene of perfect peace and solemn beauty, the stillness only being broken by the noise of falling water. The view in front of us was wild and fascinating. The angry waters of a swollen burn were shooting headlong down a precipitous cleft in the hillside ending in a dark pool below a series of waterfalls, out of which a stream rushed angrily for the space of fifty yards or so, through a funnel-shaped creek (in which we had just landed) into the salt water.

As we scrambled up the slippery rocks, we could see in the distance about two miles off to the south-east, the upper portion of the body of water which forms the Eas-Coul-Aulin, taking one sheer gigantic leap down the Leitir Dhubh Ridge, to disappear behind a projecting arm of land, which concealed the tail-end of this spectacular cataract.

All around us were dark brown masses of mountains and overhead wheeled a pair of buzzards whose wings scarcely quivered as they soared out of sight over the heights to the west of where we stood. A buzzard's flight is very eagle-like and very often the buzzard is mistaken for the eagle especially during a strong breeze which assists soaring powers. Buzzards are recognised by their high-pitched " kew-kew " cry.

In order to reach, within casting distance, the pool below the lower waterfall which thundered down a short distance in front of us, was indeed a gymnastic feat to say nothing of a risky business, as one false step would inevitably have ended in disaster.

After creeping gingerly along a perilously slimy ledge, the sound of the falling water seemed to become more and more intense and our voices seemed to grow fainter and fainter as they mingled with the crashing noise of the cascade. Finally, on rounding a huge boulder, we were suddenly confronted with one dirty-white hissing sheet of foam, the sight of which caused our nerves to tremble from the tension of keeping our balance of body and mind in this desolate place; but we pressed on steadily forward until we ultimately found shelter below another large rock above a sloping ridge, which shielded us from the spray. Under the arch of this boulder we partook of some sandwiches and a drink from our thermos flasks before commencing fishing operations.

Having refreshed ourselves, we baited our respective hooks with two or more large worms and cast our lines, which we heavily weighted with sinkers to withstand the current, into the swirling drumly pool below the place where we stood.

In the twinkling of an eye, my wife was fast into a fish which, after boring about for a time at the bottom of the pool, charged straight down-stream; but she held on doggedly while her reel screeched forth, and finally, after a terrible conflict, I netted for her in a backwater some yards farther down-stream, a sea trout of about 3 lbs.

Yes, the fish were definitely on the take, for we grew literally tired throwing back numbers of small brown and sea trout, and parrs which were undersized, and had constantly to rebait our hooks.

All of a sudden I saw my friend's rod arch and vibrate

violently in battle with something really heavy. The fish
first of all rushed madly about the pool before resting almost
stationary resisting the current.   I give my elderly companion
full credit for the steadiness and self-possession which he
displayed when he accidently slipped and tumbled with rod
in hand still playing his captive as " postie " gripped hold of
him and trailed him to safety in " the nick of time ".   Clutching
hold of the gaff, I managed with difficulty to lower myself on
to a projecting piece of rock almost at the base of the fall
and waited for breath-taking minutes until he played the fish
inshore to where I stood.   As I lunged forth to cleek it, the
fish gave a leap; but I managed, goodness knows how, to
gaff him, as if by a miracle half in mid-air.   But I lost my
balance, and the next thing I can remember was Donald
hauling me, half dazed, up the rocks still clutching the gaff-
hook, the prong of which was embedded clean through the
belly of the wriggling " beastie "—a grilse, I should say, of
some 6 lbs.

What a great revelation it would be to some of these
Thames float fishers were they to forsake the bovine com-
placency of their English placid streams for a cast in one of
our wild rushing Highland rivers.   These so-called anglers
have not lived.   They have not yet known what it means to
fish, and I strongly object to the man who dares to postulate
that fishing is a slow and tedious pastime!   And for those of
my readers who have never ventured to fish the Alt Maldie
before, may I warn them of its many dangers.   But hence
the sport!

As the light was commencing to dwindle, and as our
supply of worms was getting exhausted, notwithstanding the
mysterious beauty of our waterfall, we decided to say farewell
to the cataract, which, when we left it, as the misty twilight
was beginning to give a ghostly grandeur to our wild surroundings, seemed to be cleaving asunder the wild bold rocks
like the Archangel's glittering sword.

Yes, I must confess, having had all the sport we wanted for
one day, we longed to get out of reach of the plunge of this
awful fall, so packing up, we lost no time in getting aboard

PLATE XV

At Kyle Strome Pier, Sutherland

our boat again and pushing off from the shore, we were soon
heading in the direction of Kylesku Ferry.

I may say I was glad of the exercise to get some warmth
into my chill soaking limbs after our day's adventure.

While rowing homeward in the rays of the setting sun,
Donald's voice rang out in sublime melody, as he chanted
to the even stroke of the oars, what appeared to me to be a
most unusually beautiful and fascinating Gaelic song.

Having heard him sing it for some time, " Donald," said
I, " I am a member of An Communn Gaidhealach and
know something about Gaelic songs; but can you explain to
me what the fascinating melody is which you are singing, as
I must confess I cannot recollect having heard it before."
" O dear me," was his reply, " I did not think you would
recognise it; but it is a very simple old refrain, which can be
just as easily rendered as a rowing song, or as a lament.   It is
locally known as *Currie Dubh Nan Ropa*."   " No," I said,
" I do not seem to have ever heard it until now."   " Well some
day you will know it," said Donald with a smile, " but there
is a weird and unusual local tale concerning it, and as we
are about to land at the Hotel Ferry, there is no time to talk
about it."

As we were all wet through to the skin, and as this was our
last night at Kylesku, I invited Donald to join us in the
" Snuggery " of the Inn after supper, in order to glean from
him particulars concerning his plaintive Gaelic song.

And so, by arrangement, we met our local friend in the
Hotel as darkness was falling, when he, over a refreshment,
narrated to us the following very unusual story, which I consider is well worthy of being reproduced herewith:

CURRIE DUBH NAN ROPA
Black-haired Currie of the Rope

Many years ago, the beautiful daughter of the then Laird
of Glendhu and surrounding districts (Sutherland) fell in love
with a fierce sea-captain of the name of Currie, who belonged
to Gairloch in Ross-shire.

L

According to the legend, Currie's ship—a fishing vessel—hit a rock somewhere near Kylesku on her way into Loch Glendhu, but the skipper managed to run her aground and save her crew.   It was while waiting there for repairs that he made the acquaintance of the Laird's daughter, and their friendship quickly ripened into love.   Before Currie left Loch Glendhu for far-away ports she had promised to wait for him, and he swore to be true to her and to marry her the next time he came back on his ship to Kylesku.   They arranged to correspond regularly when he was away.

Sir J——— M——— of Achmore, Assynt, was also seeking the girl's hand in marriage and although she had no fancy at all for Sir John, her father was very anxious that she should marry him, and did his utmost to make her forget her seaman lover.

The Laird in those days had certain powers even over the mails, and was able to intercept all letters between Currie and his daughter, so that she despaired of ever seeing him again.   In her soreness of heart she is said to have sung the following song (which has since been set to music and is still a popular one in the district).*

1. Currie dubh nan ròpa
    Có bhiodh brònach uime?
    Ach b'anns' le mac an t-seòid
    Falbh le cleòc 's gunna.

Black Currie of the rope
Who would feel sorry for him?
The heart's desire of the son of the gentleman
Would be walking out with his cloak and his gun.

Chorus:
    Cadal cha dèan mi,
    Sùgradh cha dèan mise;
    Nochd cha chaidil mi.
    Tha mo luaidh a' tighinn,
    Cadal cha dèan mi.

I will not sleep
I will do no courting, I will take no pleasure;
I will not sleep to-night
My dear one is coming—
Sleep I will not.

2. Currie 's am fear bàn
    Fhuair mi gràdh bho'n dithis;
    Thug iad bhuan mo chail,
    'S chan 'eil mo shláinte fligheadh.

Currie and the fair fellow
I gave my love to both
I lost my appetite
And am now love-sick.

3. Shéid a' ghaoth o 'n tuath
    Suas an Caolas-Cumhang;
    Thug thu i mun cuairt,
    'S bhuail i air an rudha,

The wind blew from the North
Up Kylesku;
You turned her about,
And she struck on a point,

4. Bhuail i air an tràigh
Far nach d'fhàs an duileasg;
Leum thu dhith a ghràidh,
'S shàbhail thu iad uile.

She struck on the shore
Where the dulse did not grow;
You leaped out of her, my love
And you saved them all.

5. Ged gheibhinn Coille Stròm,
An tigh mór 's am fearann,
B'annsa leam bhith air bòrd
Measg nan ròp le Currie.

Although I would get the Wood of Strome
The big house and the land,
I would far rather be on board ship
Among the rope(s) with Currie.

6. Théid mi thar a' Chuirn Bhàin,
Ni mi àite suidh ann
Coimhead air an Stòr
Far an seòl na longan.

I will go on foot to Cairnbawn,
I will make a place to sit there
Looking at Stoer Head
Where the ships sail.

7. Am MacCoinnich ùr
A' togail sùil ri gunna;
Ach Currie a' Chuain tuaith,
Thug thu bhuaith' an t-urram!

The new Mackenzie (i.e. Sir John)
Is aiming his gun,
Oh, Currie in the Northern Ocean
You beat him in deserving honour!

8. Cha b'ann an sabhal feòir
Fhuair mi 'n tòs a bhruidheann,
Ach an seòmar àrd
An tigh bàn a' ghlinne.

It was not in the hay-barn
That I got the beginning of the talking
But in the high room
Of the white house of the glen.

9. B' òg a thug mi dhuit an gaol
'S daor a rinn mi cheannach;
Cha b'e gaol gun uaill
Dh'fhàg mo ghruaidhean cho tana.

It was young that I fell in love,
But it was a hard bargain;
It was not love without honour
That left my cheeks so thin.

10. Ged gheibhinn leaba ùr
'S i dèanta suas le itean
B'fheàrr leam leaba chaol
'S an darna leth aig Currie.

Though I would get a new bed,
And it made up with feathers,
I would rather have a narrow bed
And share it with Currie.

At last, however, she yielded to her father's persuasions and married Sir John.

Some time afterwards, Currie came back to Loch Glendhu and was told about the grand marriage of the Laird's daughter. Furious with anger, and determined to prove that he at least

* I managed with some considerable difficulty to jot down the words (ten verses and a chorus) of this very old local traditonal Highland song; but, being unable to read music, I could not record the weird and fascinating air; however, I took the verses and the chorus back to Edinburgh with me and quite by chance a line of one of them struck a responsive chord in the memory of one of my oldest friends from Sutherland, who remembered hearing it at his mother's knee in Elphin. He managed to record the forgotten tune (lost for nearly one hundred years) in sol-fa. I took the sol-fa setting of the tune to a well-known church organist friend who kindly reproduced and resurrected the ancient melody in staff notation. The honour of playing this tune for the first time before an Edinburgh audience, fell to Piper William Ross of the Edinburgh City Police on the occasion of a West End marriage, shortly before the last Great War broke out.

had been faithful, he shouldered his gun and set off for Achmore. When Sir John saw him approach, he fled in seeming terror, to the hills. Currie spent all that day and the next night with his former sweetheart, then set off for Kylesku.

Knowing that now she could never be his, he tried to drink himself into a state of oblivion at Kylesku Inn, and being in a fuddled condition as he left for the shore, did not notice Sir John, who having only feigned terror, had concealed himself until Currie left Achmore and had followed him to Kylesku and then shot him through the heart as he was leaving the Inn. He dragged the body up to Lochan Dubh by the road to Kylesku Post Office, and dumped the remains into the lochan (now the reservoir that supplies Kylesku Hotel with water).

He then returned to Achmore where, after shooting his faithless wife, he turned his gun on himself.

The ghost of the murdered skipper is still said to haunt Lochan Dubh; and those who have passed by Achmore late at night when the moon is full, declare that they have seen the pale wraith of the unhappy bride, and have heard the strains of her plaintive song.

And so the last night of our holiday at Kylesku came to a close; but before retiring to bed we stood outside the porch of the Hotel for a few minutes to enjoy the peaceful scene as the darkness was setting in.

The descending sun was casting its long streaks of light and shade on the scene, shadowing the sides of the mighty hills deep and motionless into the water of the loch. The mountains near and at a distance seemed, by their profound stillness, to be awaiting some awful event that was about to befall.

As far as the eye could visualise, this marine landscape of surpassing beauty and of sheer rocky precipices, formed a boundary on each side of the black water as if guarding against intrusion. Boulders of immense size loomed up, all around us, rocks which seemed to have been suddenly arrested in the act of rolling into the sea, and all traces of life seemed strangely lost, other than the plaintive cry of the night birds. In places,

immense blocks of stone piled upon and jammed into one
another, ending in the sky. Even human interest seemed
now shut out and we were brought face to face with Nature.

The air was balmy beyond description and a great calmness
reigned throughout the mountain solitude, causing grave and
strange fancies to fill our minds. The gloom was now fast
gathering round us, and as we gazed upon the bleak outline
of the tremendous crags and precipices, a sense of solemn awe
crept through us, which caused us to meditate upon our own
feebleness, which seemed to bring us into relation with God
the Creator who alone can overcome the sense of utter weak-
ness and helplessness which men must ever feel in the grasp
of such tremendous forces. Such thoughts brought back to
mind the passage: " The everlasting mountains were scattered,
the peaceful hills did bow."

All night long, the distant mountain torrents warbled their
sweetest lullabies, while we slumbered, and the gentle swell of
the tide added music to the rippling hush of the ruffled wrack
as the wavelets rose and receded, giving expression to the
words: " How wonderful are Thy works, O Lord, in wisdom
and in beauty hast Thou made them all."

CHAPTER XXI

LOCH FISHING FOR SEA TROUT

by CHARLES JEWELL

OUR GUESTS have just left for the South. Before leaving, they both urged me to write something about loch fishing for sea trout. My friends, man and wife, are widely experienced fishermen, and I had not thought much either of our fishing or its interest to the generality of anglers. However, it was pointed out to me that it was in actual fact an unusual form of sport. In England, for instance, it was unknown. My friend was doubtful as to whether it was done in Wales. And he went on to say that most sea trout fishing was done in rivers, and then usually by night.

These notes, therefore, are a summary of some fifteen years' experience of the same fishings. I am in no sort of way a student of fishing, and have kept no records beyond the Game book. I can write with fair assurance that what I have to say is correct and true about my own fishings. I wish to make it clear that I do not go beyond that. But I would risk this assertion, that Loch fishing for sea trout is decidedly not as easy as it looks.

All loch fishers, so I am told, belong to the " chuck it and chance it " class, or so they may appear in the eyes of the dry-fly expert. And indeed, one must grant that one doesn't know what one is casting over. But it would be a mistake to infer from this that catching fish in a loch is not a game of skill (like poker?).

There is also the point that one may develop a special sense. This may guide one, in some curious way, generally, that is to say, to which end of the loch or which side of the loch one should go; and, in a finer pitch of accuracy, when one may expect to be fishing over fish. I am quite definitely of opinion that this is so, and I should add that some Highland ghillies unquestionably have this ability. On a larger scale, some North Sea skippers have a marvellous sense of where to find the herring shoals. But it is not so easy to give definite proof on such a small scale as a loch.

However that may be, perhaps I should confine myself to more practical matters. The loch which I have fished most often, Loch Uisg, lies due East-and-West, about two miles long, almost straight and rather narrow in comparison with its length. It lies between steep wooded hillsides, the north side being a peak of 2,300 ft., Craig Ben, where an occasional stag is shot by the stalking members of my family. This narrow depression continues both east and west, so that the loch often has a useful breeze on it when everything else is quiet and still; but a strong wind outside becomes a howling gale, against which two strong men can make no progress whatever. The loch, in spite of its terrific sides, is extremely shallow; it has been sounded all over, and is nowhere more than twenty feet deep. The bottom is nearly all of it large stones, and the loch is remarkably clear of weeds. They do grow, however, offshore of several low bracken-covered points jutting into the loch, where burns come down from the hills. In one corner is a group of water-lillies. During winter, a number of wild swans spend many months at the lower end, where it is shallow and there is a big patch of mixed weeds. Eastwards, in the distance, framed in a gap between the hills, is the summit of Ben Cruachan; westward, Ben Buie and Beinn nan Gobhar; it is among the most beautiful places that I know.

It is connected to the sea by an artificially dug channel just over half a mile in length, a direct route. Some eighty years ago, it wandered to and fro over the levels, and joined with the big Toomeran burn, a run of about a mile or more with the windings, and entered the sea at quite a different place. The sea trout spawn partly in a tiny burn, no more than six inches wide, at the top of the loch, or they come down the burn and turn up a side burn to spawn. A few artificial croys were made some twelve years back, but I cannot trace any effect upon the fish or their habits.

The main run of fish gathers in most years in June, and granted a goodish spate starts up the burn in the last days of June. Failing a spate, the fish wait in the sea. They continue to run up during July, August and September, as one catches them in their silver livery with sea lice still on them; but the later run fish are mostly finnock. Whether there is an earlier run I do not know; I doubt it, but this year, to my surprise, I caught a fine fish in early June, so local experts may have been wrong all the time in asserting that nothing goes up before the 27th of June. Once up, they discolour rather quickly. Most years, the best fishing is between July 15th and August 15th; after that, what with bad weather, the fish getting dour and finikin, and the autumn cold approaching, we don't usually do much good.

Now, to the fishing itself. I am a bit uncomfortable, I admit, since apart from the feeling that a lot of expert fishermen will be reading what I have to say, I remember well one evening, when at half past six, my son and I saw the Minister, Mr. McIntyre, strolling along the road by the shore. We had been on the loch since morning, and had caught nothing. I lent him my rod, and out went a wonderful cat's cradle tangle, and it landed just in front of the boat close to the blade of the oar. A sea trout of over a pound promptly attached himself to the fly, and it has always puzzled me how he ever found it! To add to this, the Minister repeated the performance ten minutes later. It pleased him considerably, but left us somewhat shaken. A painful subject, and I would only say that as a rule sea trout are less easily pleased.

First, considering the matter of flies. There are two flies which I find myself always using, a Soldier Palmer on the tail and a Zulu on the dropper. Some years ago, rightly or wrongly, I succeeded in convincing myself that the fish were fussy about the Palmer. I bought them from various excellent firms, but those I bought from the Ironmonger in Oban caught fish when the others did not. They were definitely different from all the others in this respect; the hackle was slightly grizzled, giving it an old-aged look, while the hackles that didn't catch fish were a rich dark brown. Now, during the war years I was able to get away from my duties to some extent, but I was not able to be so choosy as in peace-time about Palmers. I cannot be sure if it was necessary. I can say that this year has been a wonderful year for the loch, and I have done well with the Palmer; but I have not had one single fish on it above two lbs., which seems a bit odd, as they are there. What the smaller sea trout take hardly counts. I think that if I pulled some of the wool off our black cocker and made a fly of it, it would catch them.

Here again, this is not to say that other flies do not occasionally catch good fish. Early this season, I did well with a winged fly, body iridescent green, with a gold tip, wings dark brown, the whole lightly dressed. We have often done well, and got the bigger fish, with Hardy's Loch Ordie fly, a double-barrelled affair, tandem really, but the hackle is grizzled to almost white, and instead of the red body this is dark brown, with (I believe) a very tiny sheath of cork. The method of fishing this fly is a special one, all its own, and to those who do not know it may be interesting. It fishes best in a goodish wind, needs a strong rod and heavyish line, and the fly should be doped as a dry fly. It is then thrown across the wind as far as possible, and drawn towards the boat as best possible as regards speed and direction . . . if the gale is strong it takes charge of the fly and line, and one can only draw in line. If ever fishing is a test of nerve, this method fills the bill. The big fellows come at the fly quite slowly and almost right out of the water, and usually succeed in exciting the fisherman into an immediate and wild strike, which is certain to lose the fish. But we have several fish of 3 lbs. and 4 lbs. to the credit of this fly.

The Butcher appears to be useful on certain days, though I do not remember taking any of the more sizeable fish with it. I have had a little success with a Woodcock and Olive-green, also a Woodcock and Yellow. The Peter Ross and Teal and Green have done badly, and the same applies to Black and Blae, Blue Zulu and Grouse and Claret. I have done a shade better with a smallish Mallard and Claret with blue (slightly grizzled) hackle. I have done a considerable amount of experimenting with lures, such as Daddy-longlegs, grasshoppers, coch-y-bonddhu beetles, caterpillars, demons, tiny spoons, and so forth, and whether because I hadn't enough patience or because they weren't any real good, I have returned invariably to my two favourites.

Now, since I have already raised the question of things beyond our ken in finding fish, I may digress here and raise another equally controversial point regarding a psychological question. Is it or is it not the fact that we fish better when we are fresh, and worse when we are tired? And that we fish better when we have confidence in ourselves *and our flies?*

I may add that I fish three other sea trout lochs, and one very fine and interesting hill loch where stocked Levens run to over 4 lbs., and they all vary in regard to what are good and bad flies. I should say, therefore, that in any sea trout loch the fish will have their own and a very decided preference in flies: and what it is can only be learnt by experience. I ought to add that it seems to be advisable to use small flies; in any weather they fish as well as, if not better than, medium and larger flies, and they seem to collect the biggest fish. I do prefer, however, to have the tail fly one size larger than my dropper fly.

This infers that I only use two flies; this is so. Here again I am entering the realm of speculation, but I have formed the opinion that if one puts on a cast a fly which the fish *don't* like, it will actually prevent them from or influence them against taking other flies on the cast which they *do* like. I have had a number of guests fishing with me, and I have noticed what other fishing parties were using in the other boat (there is a second boat on Uisg). But I find quite definitely that I catch fish perfectly satisfactorily with two good flies, while other anglers (whom I know to be much more expert than I am) fishing with three from the other end of my boat do not get as many or as large fish.

It is possible that this may be in part due to the difference in casts used. My own preference is the " camouflaged gut " casts made by Fosters of Ashbourne, and I use a long cast, of $3\frac{1}{2}$ yards. For what it is worth, I think they help me con-

siderably on difficult days; when there is little wind, and
that erratic in direction, or when the sun is bright. I am
inclined to think that the size of gut as sold by different firms
varies, for instance Foster's gut appears to me to be on the
thin side, while Malloch's is on the thick side. I am inclined
to think that the size of gut makes quite a big difference to
one's success; on a windy day, it is true, one can use thicker
gut, but even at that I find it always pays to use the thinnest
possible size of gut. I find Foster $3 \times$ the lightest, as we get
fish of over 4 lbs. and most of them are, like Alan Breck,
bonnie fighters. On the roughest days, I find $1 \times$, if anything,
too heavy, though the cast lasts longer. No doubt it is the
general experience; but I find that, with a light cast, after
one has had two stiff tussles with good fish, or a really long
and hard struggle with a fish, the gut is so weakened that it is
useless. I have often been guilty of carrying on too long
with weakened casts, for the sake of economy. It is no
economy, even in peace time, for the loss of one two-pounder
offsets the cost of a new cast, quite apart from other con-
siderations.

It follows that if I recommend the use of $3 \times$ gut for gentle
days, and thin $3 \times$ at that, the rod must not be too heavy,
and the strike must be done just right. Now I know nothing
about rods, and would just mention that my own is a Hardy
Palakona " Perfection ", 9 ft. 6 ins., which I found twenty
years ago at Vaughan's, and distinctly second-hand. This is
only strong enough for big sea trout if one has plenty of backing
on the reel, a clever ghillie at the oars, and a loch without
weed in it. Equally, it is too strong for finnock, and for these
a " Casting Club de France " will give more sport. And I
should say that there is no real need to go beyond $2 \times$ unless
one is using a heavier rod, and even then a little extra care in
striking should enable this strength of gut to be used even
where an occasional grilse is found. And $1 \times$ is nearly always
too heavy, except for wild days. I have sometimes suspected
that after some length of use the camouflaged gut has an
adverse effect on the fish in the $1 \times$ size, but this does not
apply to the $2 \times$ and smaller sizes.

Now, I have mentioned that the strike must be just right. After all these years of experience of sea trout I am reluctant to attempt any dissertation on the subject of how to strike sea trout. I am also aware that it is a highly controversial subject. So I shall set out my own experience, for what it may be worth.

First and foremost, I am of opinion that the majority of sea trout are missed by striking quickly. I find that what pays best is either a slow strike . . . very slow! . . . or no strike at all. I do not know whether this " no strike at all " idea will be considered as fantastic or the regular thing, because, as I say, I know little of other people's fishings or their experiences. But we have had a number of our big fish without striking. Generally speaking, I find that one should avoid rigorously any strike at the " boil "; instead, one must wait until one feels the fish going down through the water with a good, healthy pull on the line . . . and *then* strike. If, however, one is used to lightning strikes (which I have found necessary for brown trout in Loch Awe and else-where), it requires iron self-discipline to unlearn this habit. Particularly since some sea trout come at the fly like an angry express-train, with the result that all one's instincts compel one to a violent and prompt reaction. This, I find, is a most reliable means of losing all the sizeable fish. It is true that if one uses a very slow strike, it is not infallible; but as we all know who fish, there is no such thing as infallibility in fishing, and it is the next best thing. I should put the best minimum time to wait before striking as two good seconds after seeing the boil . . . if one has to strike by judging the moment from it. I say " if ", because I am of opinion that the boil is a bad guide. If one possesses the necessary self-control, I feel sure that it is better to ignore the boil altogether unless it is a surface boil and the fish has seized the fly; and to go entirely by the steady pull on the line, and then strike. The boil by itself does *not* necessarily indicate that the fish has taken the fly. For, granted certain conditions, sea trout, and more especially the bigger fish, will come and inspect the fly, and leave it. If one has acted hastily, and struck, the fly will be swept away from the fish, who is naturally enough surprised at its Maskelyne-and-Devant behaviour, and will not come again. On the other hand, if one continues the gentle movement of the fly . . . or, indeed, far better, leaves the fly absolutely motionless for a few seconds and then continues the movement . . . and subsequently, having shortened the line, drops the fly into the place where the boil appeared, it is fifty-fifty that the fish will rise again to it and take it. I have even hooked an inquisitive fish on the *fourth* cast.

It may be objected that, with the boat drifting down wind, it is impossible to make a fourth cast over the same spot. If one fishes with a normal length of line and a light rod and short cast, this is so. My own preference is definitely for a longish line, which enables one to do this if the boat is not drifting fast before a strong wind. In fact, I should say that there is almost everything in favour of fishing with a longish line, except in rare conditions, such as a dark day with a strongish breeze.

First and foremost, it gives one the ability to recast over the same spot, as I have described. Secondly, the line being longer, there is a slight delay between the act of striking and the effect of it reaching the fly. Thirdly, in certain conditions of light, when one has the sun even moderately low at one's back, I am convinced that the fish are scared by what they see of the movements of one's arms, etcetera, if one is standing up, and they will not come near the boat when they see its shadow looming down upon them as it drifts; and this, I believe, applies strongly in shallower water, say seven feet and less. Being able to fish a longish line as a habit will overcome this difficulty. One can, of course, throw the line well out at an angle, but this has its objections when two anglers are sharing a boat, since they are both facing outwards and away from each other, and a tangling of lines upwind while back-casting is inevitable. Also, I have found much greater difficulty in getting the fly to take a firm hold in a fish when casting a wide angle. Nevertheless, it does enable one to catch some fish in conditions where a short line cast straight down wind will never raise anything.

Now, I am not in favour of a *very* long line. In my experience, it is apt to lose the bigger fish. But even a longish
line provides difficulties in management. Without using
one's other hand to pull in line, one cannot fish the fly more
than a short distance without being compelled to start the
back-cast. I find that fishing the fly very slowly over a long
distance adds very considerably not only to the number of
the fish in the bag but to their quality. Bigger fish often
follow the fly quite a long way, before making up their minds
to have a go at it. Moreover, they will make this attempt
at precisely the moment when one is lifting the line for the
back-cast. Evidently, thinking they had a sure thing, they
didn't trouble; but when it started moving quicker, they
decided they had better move too! I have developed the
trick of giving it a special little jerk at the last moment and
stopping it again, just before making the back-cast. But the
fact remains that one cannot fish this slow fly over a long
distance without taking in quite a length of line by hand.
And this involves a strike off the hand, not off the reel. Except, indeed, if the fish comes at the fly when it lands on the
water. This happens often enough, by the way. I have
often been amazed at the apparent ability of the sea trout to
spot the fly in the air and take it half-volley. This applies
to the bigger fish even more than to the finnock! But I do
notice that my dry-fly expert friends throw a much prettier
line than I do. Their flies touch the water before the line;
in my case, unless I do one false cast, and am extra careful to
cast well above the surface of the water, my line lands well
before the flies. It doesn't seem to prevent my catching fish,
but I suspect that if I were a neater caster I might have
caught more!

Now besides using this slow draw with a longish line, I
try to get the point of my rod high enough to make the Zulu
dropper run along, and even bounce above, the surface of the
water. I suppose this is what is meant by " dapping " as
done on Lough Corrib, though what the sea trout think the
fly is I have no notion. The fact remains that many of our
biggest fish seem to be strongly attracted by it. Moreover,

they seem to me not only to be attracted into taking the Zulu dropper thus dapped, but they may be lured up into enquiring into it and then they decide, as an alternative, to take the Palmer that follows, albeit at some five feet distance, behind. But I find it a most difficult method; and if one is not absolutely concentrated on the task, or if one is tired or edgy, one fails to hit off the precise moment for an ideal strike; usually one loses one's head and strikes immediately . . . and there goes another big fish missed.

On account of the difficulty of this method, and for other reasons, I don't always use it. Other reasons are that sea trout, while keeping to no set rules, do vary very much in their habits. I remember very clearly one year when all the fish were about twice as plump as usual. Instead of being on the slim side, they were stocky and deep; extra well fed, no doubt. But, instead, as one might expect, of being extra strong and savage takers, they came at the Palmer when it was sunk as low as I could manage to sink it. Indeed, often the first thing one noticed was the line straightening, and a second or so later a large flat boil. They were usually well hooked however, and fought superbly.

Equally, I find that the time of day makes a difference, more especially as the season gets on. Fish during the afternoon hours are hard to raise. Then, when they do take, even a carefully delayed and apparently perfectly-timed strike will not hook them properly. I have noticed this during this present season, when my expert friend failed to connect properly with quite a number of such fish. Some were never hooked; others apparently well-hooked played for a while and then got off unaccountably. With considerable diffidence, I suggest that the fish does not take the fly thoroughly into its mouth at this time of day, when this phenomenon is in evidence. It may be that they are foul-hooked, but I do not think so, as foul-hooked fish are more often than not exceedingly well hooked, and it is only the afternoon fish that show this peculiarity. Moreover, they are apt to come up, look at the fly, and think better of it, at this time of day. I suspect that they educate themselves thereby. As a matter

of fact, I have known seasons when all the fish had a habit
of rising short, even if I left the fly motionless in the water
for them to take.

This reminds me that sea trout do not seem to get
" educated " up to the standard of the brown trout in the
dry-fly streams of southern England. I have lost a fly in a
fish one afternoon, and have hooked and landed him the next
morning. I played a three-pounder for a long time one
afternoon, and the rival firm in the second boat hooked him
and landed him the next day. I cannot swear he was the
same fish. But he was the only big one at that exact spot.

Do fish remain at fixed spots ? Well, I find that this is
one of the most fascinating points in loch fishing for sea trout
. . . and no doubt brown trout as well. I am convinced
that they do. One of my ghillies says that he thinks they
not only like certain spots, but that one fish will fight another
in order to obtain a special spot. I have seen a brown trout
of some six ounces seize a tiny fellow by the throat, and shake
him like a terrier does a rat (the little fellow was lucky, and
took his chance during an instant's carelessness on the part
of his assailant to escape); and I cannot imagine that the
sharp and business-like teeth which the sea trout develops are
merely ornamental. So the ghillie may be right. But the
fact remains that certain places are good in certain years.

As the shores of a loch wind in and out, the underwater
levels will roughly correspond. Particularly where burns run
in, a low bracken-covered point, sometimes grassed, sometimes
rather stony, will be formed, and off shore this may extend,
irregularly, quite a distance out. In Uisg, while the fishing
off these points is usually very good, this is not an invariable
rule. And I find some specially good spots off a " point "
that is so slightly projected forward as hardly to be recognised
as a " point " at all. I find, too, that where the shore is solid
rock and there is deep water directly off it, some stretches are
good and others useless. I suspect that the good spots may
have, occasionally, a largish boulder down below or, more
often, a good field of view on both sides of the point. Fish
will lie, generally, at varying distances from the shore in

accordance with weather and other conditions; and, at the various good lies, some of these are close to the shore while others are far out. Off two rather wide and prominent bracken points I find the biggest fish lie as much as fifty yards or more off the shore, habitually. On the other hand, along one of my best drifts I do not remember ever raising a fish more than some fifteen yards from shore, or twenty at the very most. Still more oddly, there is one patch in the middle of the loch, quite two hundred yards from the nearest shore, where smaller sea trout seem to frequent regularly and in fair number for no apparent reason. There is another patch much the same distance out, but in this case it is near the head of the loch and the spawning burn and I think that fish may lie all over this end. But, while drifts will vary very much from one year to another, it is correct to say that it takes a long time and close attention to learn where the sea trout in Loch Uisg are to be found. I should say that the same thing must apply to other similar lochs. Indeed, it has often been said to me that such and such a loch holds sea trout, but " they never take." I might reply that nobody thought Uisg was any good for them; and that the truth of the matter is that they are taking fish, but haven't been given the right fly in the right way at the right time at the right place.

This reminds me that there is some sort of a rule about using bright flies for bright days; and another says bright flies for dull days. For all I know, they may each of them be perfectly correct for certain lochs or rivers. But neither applies to Uisg, as far as I can judge. Otherwise, I feel sure that the Butcher would have had far more success, the more so since Uisg is full of sticklebacks. It is odd that the brownies in Uisg are most of them eight to the lb. I should have expected them, with all the vast room available, to have grown into monsters. The loch was stocked with Levens about 1928, and I have caught fish which seem to be either the stocked fish or their descendants; but my record is a 1 lb. 13 oz. fish caught this season, so they appear to be very short of feed.

M

As to the very vexed question of what is good fishing weather, I am as wise to-day as when I started.   I have known many a perfect fishing day when we caught nothing. When a north-west blows in squalls, a notoriously beastly wind hostile to all sport, the loch's surface is a confused mixture of flat calms, whirlwinds on a small scale, and definite winds in all directions at once.   Admitting this sort of day is usually bad, it is by no means a sure bet that it is.   Moreover, on the bad days, it is often the biggest fish that will be on the move, and one four-pounder is worth any amount of finnock.   And it is a feature of Uisg that even on the worst day there will be just one fish lunatic enough to come up and seize the fly, and thereby help to fill the larder for one meal.   Again, as regards temperature of the water: one of our best afternoons was after a hot spell; the water was very warm, and the wind was icy.   I do find that when the loch is very low, or very high, the fish behave oddly, often being sluggish.   And in a steady downpour of rain they will not take at all, when it has settled down to a real wet day.   But the point of the " mist being down on the hills " I find has no application whatsoever. Indeed, I have fished my hill loch for brown trout, which is over a thousand feet above sea level, with the mist just down to sea level, when I could only see the shore from five yards away, and have made an excellent bag.   I have made my record bag in an East wind.   I have caught the biggest fish on days when the wind went round in circles.   In fact, short of a flat calm or the real monsoon rain, there is no weather in which I would not hope to catch a fish.   This may not apply to lochs other than Uisg.

I have tried night fishing without success, but this doesn't prove anything, as I didn't repeat the experiment.   I think it might pay to try at dusk, both sun and moon, but haven't tried myself.   The fish have always seemed to me to go right off around half past six of an evening, but that may be wishful thinking due to the proximity of dinner ashore.

As this seems to me to have covered the ground theoretically, I think I have done enough.   Perhaps one individual experience may round off this article.   I have read many fishing books, and the one I have liked best is Negley Farson's *Going Fishing*, for the reason that he has no shame in telling everybody about the big fish he lost and why he lost them. A fellow feeling, etc. . . One morning, about the last cast before going home, I had done no good at all, and threw a fly into some very shallow water where I had never even seen a fish before. It was a windy day and I was fishing alone, with a youngster rowing, not my own professional ghillie. And there in perhaps twelve inches of water I hooked a fish. It went off steadily, and we rowed away from the shore to keep near it. I found that I had no control over it. After a quarter of an hour under water, it came near the top, and from what I saw I thought to myself, a two-pounder, and must be foul-hooked to pull so hard and so untiringly. Five minutes later I had a shock. The fish came to the surface sufficiently for me to see that what I had thought was the tail was in fact the dorsal fin, and I was attached to a monster of the deep. As the fish tired, I got it alongside the boat. I could not trust the lad even to attempt landing it with my net; each time I got it near the boat, it gave a flick of its tail and away it went. I have no idea how many times I got it almost up to the net like this, but it must have been well over twenty times, and each time the fish was more and more exhausted. And then the hook came out of its mouth. I can still see the fish, completely " out ", motionless in the water like a stuffed fish in a glass case, slowly, very slowly, sinking from the surface into the depths.

CHAPTER XXII

THE FRESH WATER EEL

by R. MACDONALD ROBERTSON

THE COMMON EEL (*Anguilla vulgaris*) in Scotland is generally regarded as a worthless creature, but this is quite erroneous, especially in time of national emergency. The Loch Lomond Angling Improvement Association, for example, I am informed, recently marketed eels to the extent of nearly £500 in a season.

Apart from its ordinary food value, from the eel can be manufactured *inter alia*, fats, margarine, invalid foods, medical oils (both for internal and external use), lubricating oils, burning oils, glycerine, explosive substances, glue gelatine and from the skin, bandages for sprains, etc.

FOOD VALUE OF THE EEL

	Water per cent.	Protein per cent.	Fat per cent.	Fuel Value (Calories per lb.)
Eel - - - - -	59·8	13·75	25·69	1339
Salmon - - - -	61·4	17·73	20·00	1173
Herring - - - -	72·5	19·5	7·1	660
Halibut - - - -	75·4	18·7	5·2	565

The eel is a highly nutritive food for poultry. At practically no expense—bar the catching—eels, through simple process of manufacture, can be made into a valuable fish and meal diet for hens, etc. In remoter Highland country districts, eels are boiled up for food for poultry by the crofters.

Hundreds of tons of elvers visit and mature in British rivers yearly; but only a limited proportion are captured. Norfolk fishers have been known to make hauls from 100 lbs. to 400 lbs. in a night.

To rid our Scottish waters of eels would materially improve

spawning in our rivers and lochs. Being voracious creatures, eels are a pestilence and the destruction wrought by them on other fish is tremendous especially upon the " redds " of brown trout, but eels do not readily get the same opportunity of devouring the " redds " of salmon and sea trout as, owing to a dispensation of nature, the inset of colder weather with the advancement of autumn, causes the eels to retire to winter quarters where they hibernate and are thus out of the way before spawning begins.

There are far greater numbers of eels per acre in this country than one would imagine. Summer eels (yellow-bellied type) feed mostly on shrimps and fry. The belly of an eel turns yellow or silver coloured according to age, sex and time of year, but the only real or noticeable change of colour takes place when the eel completes its second meta-morphosis in preparation of its long sea voyage to the spawning grounds. It then becomes definitely silver-coloured as the body openings close when the eel takes on all the characteristics of the deep sea fish. There are two types of eel in this country, known as snub-snout and sharp-pointed-snout eels; but actually these are the same species of fish, as there is only one species of fresh-water eel in European waters.

While fishing Loch Ness I observed a salmon of about 18 lbs. lying dead a few yards away from where my boat was anchored in shallow water near the bank. When I lifted it out of the water I found a hole in its side near the tail. On squeezing the side of the fish I felt a distinct movement and, to my surprise, three eels wriggled their way out of the wound. Perhaps these creatures might have been lampreys (*Petromyzon marinus*) but I must confess I did not pay particular attention at the time as I was eager to proceed with the day's fishing. They had evidently eaten their way inside the fish under its skin. I learned from my ghillie that eels have been known to attack salmon (when in a " spent " condition) and on entering their inside, commence operations by devouring the entrail first and then the flesh.

On another occasion, on looking over the Dulnain Bridge (near Grantown-on-Spey) one morning when the water was

low, I observed a salmon of about 8 lbs. lying dead at the
bottom of the pool below.   From where I stood, I could see a
number of eels preying on it.   But an eel will not attack a
salmon unless the latter is bleeding as the result of an injury
and far " spent ".   Fresh blood attracts eels more than anything else—they follow the scent.

In autumn most burns yield a good run of eels.   Only
migratory eels, i.e. Silver Eels, make for the salt water in September and early October; others hibernate.   Eels are to be
found in the most secluded pools and ditches in our country.
Eels are even known to have been caught in streams above the
Falls of Glomach in Ross-shire, which have more or less a
precipitous descent of some 365 feet.   Hence the mystery—
however can they reach this level since they hail from the sea?
But although the eel is a fish and its proper place is in the
water, it can come out of the water and take short cuts overland.
Eels possess a water-carrying apparatus, which accounts for
their extraordinary tenacity of life and enables them to travel
overland for considerable distances when there is sufficient
moisture to permit them to do so, for, if they dry, they die in
a comparatively short space of time.   The water is stored in
the eel's gill cavity.

The problem of the generation of the eel is most abstruse
and very curious; but it has been established that there are
two migrations of eels—one up and one down rivers, one
from and the other to the sea; the first in spring and summer,
and the second in autumn and early winter.   (Small eels,
often not more than $2\frac{1}{2}$ ins. long in the first place and in the
second place 3 or 4 ft. long—weight up to 20 lbs.)

Eels found in fresh water are the result of the first migration.
They appear in millions in springtime.   About the end of
July, some years ago, while visiting the Falls of Tummel,
Perthshire, I observed that the water was blackened by millions
of little elvers constantly urging their way up the slimy rocks
by the side of the falls.   Thousands died, but their bodies,
remaining moist, served as ladders for others to make their
way up stream, ascending actually perpendicular rocks, conducting their journey through wet moss or adhering to some

other of their kind which had succumbed in their attempt. Such is the energy of these little creatures, as they continue to wend their way in immense numbers up stream.

While eels can pass by moss, and mount rocks, they fail to penetrate limestone (or any other rock not having holes or clefts) or move against a rapid descending current of water.

When eels enter into confined water they fatten and thrive there if sufficient food is present.

It is difficult to reason as to the instinct which leads young eels to seek fresh water. Probably they prefer warmth and swimming at the surface in early summer, find the lighter water warmer and likewise containing more grubs and insects and thus pursue the courses of fresh water, as the waters from the land, at this season, become warmer than those of the sea.

When cold water from the autumnal floods begins to swell the rivers, eels on their spawning migration endeavour to return to the salt water on their final journey in the form of Silver Eels; but numbers of the smaller unmatured ones conceal themselves in mud during winter, massed together for warmth. All eels, not migrating, hibernate during winter unless conditions are very warm. There are distinct accounts of small eels rising up flood-gates and posts of water works, such as those of the Caledonian Canal. They have been known to make their way to higher water levels though the boards were smooth planes and five or six feet perpendicular.

When they first rise out of the water upon the dry board, they rest a little until their slime is exhausted and sufficiently glutinous—and then they rise up the perpendicular ascent with the same facility as if they had been moving on a surface plane, assisted by their small scales, which placed like those of the snake, facilitate their progressive motion. Eels grow, feed and fatten in fresh water. In small streams they attain no great length, but in lochs they become large and often as thick as a man's arm. All those of considerable proportion (in the final migration stage as spawning or Silver Eels) attempt to return to the sea in " the Back End ", probably when they experience the chill autumnal climate; but those that are not of the largest proportions, pass the winter in the mud of lochs and rivers and, without eating, remain torpid.

The increase in the size of the eel is not certainly known in any given period of time; but depends upon the quantity of their food.

Large eels, having migrated to salt water, never return to fresh water again.

A fresh-water eel contained in a glass tank in a museum grew to an extraordinary size. On attaining its eighth year it became tremendously active and, by some impulse or other, escaped. It was discovered some time afterwards, a fair distance away, heading directly towards the sea (i.e. the salt water nearest the place of its captivity).

Actually, eels do comparatively little active swimming. They delight to wriggle through mud or in and out of holes and crevices.

The Lamprey, or the Lampern (*Petromyzon fluviatlis*), derived from the Latin word " stone " and " to suck ", refers to the habit of attaching to stones by its suckerlike mouth. These creatures enter British rivers for spawning, and seldom reach a length of more than three feet.

An eel which has been taken out of the water will appear to have a swelling on each side of its throat, due to the supply of water in the gill cavities. Eels come out of their hiding holes and roam more freely during the dark hours than in the daytime, especially when the grass is moist. Further, eels have a natural homing instinct and will always take the nearest and most direct course back to the water from which they have been captured.

The following are perhaps the easiest and most inexpensive methods of capturing eels, which add to the country's food supply:

Eel Weirs.—These are used in rivers and their main purpose is to interrupt descending fish and concentrate them into the openings called " eel eyes ", where the nets are set. Long conical coghill nets are used in the " eel eyes ", usually from thirty to sixty feet in length. The mesh is $2\frac{1}{2}$ knot at the mouth of the net and is reduced to $\frac{1}{2}$ knot at the tail. Eels migrate in September and October and usually choose a dark and stormy night for the purpose. Great hauls are got in this way, especially in Ireland, where this type of fishing is a considerable industry.

Long Lines.—This method is best suited to lochs. Lines may be almost any length convenient to handle. The snoods (short lengths of line with hooks attached fastened to the main line) are placed about six feet apart. The snoods should be about six feet long to prevent the eels entangling the snoods in the line. Bait may be earthworm, young fish, raw ox-liver, etc., or even parts of eels themselves. Time for lining is from spring to late summer.

Eel Traps or Eel Picks are used for picking up eels from weeds and mud and are usually in the form of a wire basket, either with two mouths or with one mouth and the opposite end covered with sacking, to the inner side of which the bait is attached. The sacking can be easily removed for the release of the eels and for cleaning. Traps may be fished from May to September.

Eel Buck.—A wooden framework supporting a number of wicker baskets which are lowered below the surface of the water to catch the eels.

Eel Pot.—A kind of basket with a funnel-shaped mouth used for catching eels. They force their way in but cannot get out.

Eel Set.—A special type of net designed for catching eels. It is set across a sluggish stream or river—the sharp-nosed eels being the kind generally caught.

Babbing is a term used for worming eels. The Bab is made by threading worms on worsted strands two to three feet in length firmly secured with string, attached to a pole. The cluster of worms is danced up and down in the water to attract the eels. When the teeth of the eel get stuck into the worms, it can easily be lifted out of the water. By babbing, thousands of eels can be taken during the months of May and June, where bream, roach and rudd spawn.

Eel Nets (Dutch).—With 60 to 80 nets great hauls can be taken. There are two kinds of nets known respectively as the Single Winger and the Double Winger.

Packing for Market.—Eels, to fetch the best price, must

arrive at the place of sale not merely alive, but actually lively. Feeding eels should be kept in a " live box " or eel trunk (a large perforated box placed under the water in which live eels are kept) for several days, to allow all the remains of food to be discharged from the stomach and gut, and for the eels to " harden " as the saleswomen term it.   The eels should then be packed in shallow boxes or in boxes containing a number of shallow trays, in such a way that there is practically only a single layer of fish in the box or tray.   Eels must not be crowded on top of one another or they will die in their own slime.   If the weather is hot the top tray in a case of eels should contain ice, the water from which drips down through the other trays.   The best box is 2½ feet long by 2 feet wide and contains four trays each about 3 inches deep.   Eels are sold by the draught of 21 lbs.   The average weight of an eel is 17 ounces.   There is a keen market for eels in England, and Billingsgate is the best market.

The majority of Scottish anglers regard eels as a thoroughly disagreeable nuisance as they entangle the line in a most amazing way, if allowed to; but if, when an eel is landed, it is laid down upon a newspaper, to which it sticks, it can be dealt with more easily.   Eels as a rule have an irritating way of taking when not wanted and, after being hooked, show a reprehensible unwillingness to come to land and no other fish sulks with greater skill or determination.   If permitted time, the eel bores into the mud or twists the line round a tree root which makes it very difficult to avoid broken tackle.   If brought coiling to the shore, it will frequently be discovered that the eel has gorged the bait, and some fishers, rather than undertake the messy task of dissection, cut the gut and resign themselves to the loss of a hook.   By using a double-hook, much of this trouble can be averted, as the tackle does not usually get much farther than its mouth, as the eel is usually caught by the lip, from which the hook can be disengaged without trouble.   When a hooked eel twists itself round some obstruction in the water, he cannot readily be wrenched out of such a position; but an eel cannot maintain its hold for very long against a steady strain on the line pulling at his mouth and finally allows himself to be dragged to the bank, As a boy I used to enjoy spearing eels. The deadliest kind of spear is actually not a spear at all, but resembles a pair of large shears with toothed blades to hold the slimy fish. The eel emerges from its hiding place more freely at night than in the day time, and is according to this method more effectively caught by torchlight. A clear rippling burn is best for the purpose and more than one person should take part in the operation. On many an occasion I have waded up the " Claddach " of a stream clad in an old kilt, while participating in this picturesque amusement. A torch enables the fisherman to observe everything clearly on the bottom of the water, from little stones to grains of sand. Save for the quiver of their fins as they breast the current, the dark forms of salmon and trout appear almost motionless, and the fish are not a bit afraid. Eel spearing can make a most convenient cloak for less innocent practices. Where salmon and large trout are to be found, the deadly leister is often substituted for the harmless pair of shears, but one should always bear in mind that mere killing is not true sport.

Although much information has been gleaned of recent years about the life history of the fresh water eel, it still remains an amazing fact that these common fresh-water creatures are born thousands of feet deep in the warm waters of the Sargasso Sea—Atlantic Ocean—some 3,000 miles from Britain, yet swim slowly to some destined riverway in our little Island, where they dwell for a considerable number of years in the streams of their choice, until they are impelled to obey Nature's command to increase and multiply, when they travel by night on their great adventure to the far-off West Indies, to deposit their ova and die. In conclusion, the eel is different from other fishes; it behaves in a singular way. It is *catadromous*, i.e., it descends to the sea to spawn, and is thus in direct contrast to the salmon, which ascends rivers to spawn, and is therefore *anadromous*. In other words, the eel is a sea fish which has learned to feed and mature in fresh water, while the salmon is a fresh-water fish which seeks its food in the abundant pastures of the salt water.

CHAPTER XXIII

THE SALT WATER EEL

by R. MACDONALD ROBERTSON

IN THE Scottish Highlands the natives, as a rule, will not eat congers on account of the resemblance in form to " . . . . the kin of the serpent once wrought all ill to nurse the bond of earthly evil," and frequently they are inclined to discourage fishing for them, notwithstanding that there is a considerable market for congers in English towns.

The conger, like the common fresh-water eel, provides a highly nutritious and reasonably priced food. The flesh resembles that of Ling (*Molva vulgaris*) but contains a greater proportion of ossified tissue. Elongated fishes, like the eel, move with great speed by rapid undulations of the body. The forward motion is effected by the pressure of the body against the water, enclosed in the several incurved planes arising from the undulations. Certain snakes, by adopting an entirely aquatic existence, have become quite eel-like in form rendering it very difficult to distinguish eel from snake.

Although the *Anguillae*, or fresh-water eels, belong to the family *Muraenidae*, a group of soft-rayed osseous fishes, the name also applies to other genera, notably the conger which lives in the sea. The fresh-water eel has small transparent scales embedded in its skin generally obscured with slime. The salt-water eel (conger) has no scales. The genus *Anguilla* contains twenty-five known species, two of which are looked upon as natives of the United Kingdom.

As already mentioned, the conger-eel (*Conger vulgaris*) belongs to the family of *Muraenidae*, and its life history has some points of great interest. In the past, certain small ribbon-shaped fishes caught in the Atlantic and the Mediterranean proved a puzzle to naturalists, who named them *Leptocephali*

PLATE XVI

A Night with the Congers

and supposed them to be larval forms; but within recent years research by the Italian zoologists, Grassi and Calandruccio, showed that these small fish were the larvae of the conger and other eels, now known by scientists to be the young of the conger termed *Leptocephalus morrisii*—a pale transparent phantom, like a mere strip of tape.

It is now known that the conger retreats to very deep water —probably far below the 100 fathom line—at the time of spawning, and it is understood that spawning takes place only once in a lifetime and is fatal to both parents.

It is still a matter of conjecture what becomes of the conger during the winter months; but it is possible that many of them remain close to shore in places where the temperature of the water does not fall to any great extent, and that none of them, with the exception of those that retire to spawn and die, go to a great distance. The comparative smallness of the eyes militate against the theory that they inhabit very deep water for long periods.

The conger is a rapacious creature and is classed as a salt-water scavenger. Fresh herring is perhaps the best bait for line fishing. The colour of the conger eel is generally paler than that of the fresh-water eel ; but in the Atlantic, pale congers are found on one side of the Wolf Rock and dark ones on the other.

The conger has breathing tubes, similar to the fresh-water kind. Congers possess great strength and extraordinary tenacity of life and can cause much havoc to fishing nets.

The men of Loch Awe were supposed to have been afraid of the eels of Loch Edive (Etive) which were reputed " also as big as one horse with ane certain incredible length ".

Conger eels often obtain a length up to ten feet and have been known to turn the scales at over one hundred pounds weight. These fish are common in many parts of our shores and have a preference for rocky coasts where they lie among the tangle and occasionally they are left in rock pools by the receding tides. They are capable of inflicting serious injuries with their powerful jaws and even smaller specimens should be treated with caution. I think it right to warn my readers of the dangers of wading or bathing in tidal waters against the unexpected attacks of conger eels which are particularly vicious and have a distinctly dangerous bite which usually takes a long time to heal.   I have witnessed the heel of a fisherman's boot being bitten in half by a conger.

One summer evening a big conger was caught on a set line in Loch Duich.   It was so large as to baffle two strong fishermen to get it into their boat, from which it broke away after knocking one of them overboard.   On another occasion a mighty conger eel was caught on a set line by some fishermen at the mouth of the Grimersta River on the west Coast of Lewis.   With considerable difficulty it was hauled ashore and clubbed and ultimately cut through the middle.   One fisherman took home the tail portion (grand meat for his hens) and the other the head portion.   The fisherman who removed the head portion deposited it in a barrel overnight.   In the morning he grabbed it with his right hand, when with a single snap of its jaws the conger bit off his thumb and two fingers.

In Loch Broom, a gull swooped down to the surface of the water as a conger eel glided up from the depths and in no time the bird and the fish were in deadly combat.   The conger snapped its jaws over the gull's head, the bird beating its wings to get free.   For many minutes the battle lasted and when both were captured and taken aboard a boat, the bird's head was still in the fish's mouth and both were in an exhausted condition.

It is not difficult to hook a conger eel as they are among the greediest fish which frequent our Scottish coasts; but it is quite another thing to land one especially if it be a big one.

The male conger hardly ever exceeds a length of 2 feet and a weight of $\frac{1}{2}$ lb., whereas the female reaches 50 lbs. to 60 lbs. and has been known to turn the scales above 100 lbs.

The great bulk of our salt-water fishes are wholly carnivorous and devour such marine animals as they are able to tear from their hiding places or overcome by superior strength and speed.

Very good congers are usually to be found lurking about

in deep harbours among the foundations, which can be fished for in the evening with strong stiff wiry tackle and the assistance of a lad in a dinghy to help in saving the fish; for they cannot, of course, be reeled up a jetty by brute force.

The favourite food of the conger is the octopus. Congers, like many bottom-feeders, are catholic in their tastes, and the best baits are unquestionably " cuttle " (heads for choice), mackerel and pilchard; but the bait must be fresh as the conger is a clean feeder. The bait must not be too hard for congers do not appreciate hard things in their mouths.

Congers are nocturnal in their habits, wandering forth from their lairs throughout the night over reefs and sands. They seldom take a bait by day unless dangled down within easy reach of their noses. They usually come on the feed as darkness sets in, and again just before day-break.

The usual manner of conger-fishing is to " shoot a boulter " (a long line baited with from 50 to 400 hooks). The boulter should be shot at nightfall and hauled in some four hours afterwards. That there are many congers roaming about on the sands at night is evident from the large catches made by trawlers in the regions on the west coast of Scotland. The conger is frequently to be found within hulls of ancient sunken wrecks in the cavities of which they take up their abode; but, in fact, these fishes are to be found all round our coasts and on the shores of contintental Europe; in the Atlantic and Mediterranean, along the coast of the United States, Japan and Tasmania and elsewhere.

Conger-fishing with rod affords many a thrill as well as a big tussle; but the bite of the conger is more clearly felt on a hand-line than with rod tackle. In rod fishing, very strong tackle is essential, for a large conger is tremendously powerful and knows no fatigue in fight. The killing is no easy matter, for such fish, in addition to their great strength, possess high muscular development and a very nasty mouth of teeth, together with a tail, which is the " business end ", which can be hitched on to any obstacle which presents itself within easy reach, even the keel of the boat itself, which makes it very difficult to haul her aboard; and when in the boat, if she can squirm her tail over the gunwale, she is capable of vaulting by its aid into the water again. When entrapped in a lobster-pot, for example, it is with her tail that a conger forces her way out by forcing the withes apart until she is able to gradually worm her body backwards to freedom.

For conger fishing from a boat the rod must be strong but not necessarily stiff—anything between seven to nine feet in length. The reel should be of the easy-running sea type. A lead should be attached to the line. If a boom is used it should be short, with a swivel attached to the buckle, and the lead should be simply tied on with some thin snoodings. Traces should be of wire about $1\frac{1}{2}$ yards long. Swivels should be attached to the wire snood of the hook, of good size and long-shanked hooks should be fitted, as the conger is unable to bite through wire connections. The cast should be delivered seawards so that the line falls towards the boat in going down; then reel up gently when the lure finds bottom, until the line is drawn taut between the sinker and the rod-point. Do not strike until a heavy draw is felt. Then reel up as quickly as possible in order to take the conger by surprise and get her off the bottom before she has time to hitch her tail round a rock. After that the fight will begin. Keep a steady strain on the line. The conger in fighting for its life always swims backwards (and rarely takes a head first run or a plunge to get away) much in the manner of a bull-terrier. When alongside the boat, the eel should, if possible, be gaffed through the belly as only a very strong gaff can resist the strain (for a conger can spin round and twist) if she is gaffed through the head.

A piece of the tail end of a small male conger makes quite a good bait for the larger species of this fish.

In conclusion, congers, being clean-feeding creatures, much more so than fresh-water eels, form a valuable food to large numbers of people. Anyone who eats the flesh of a conger eel gets the net benefit of lobsters, crabs and shoals of all sorts of other fish, which have built up the sinuous muscles of this rocky water terror.